ENDORSEMENT

GREAT PEOPLE ARE not those who hail from affluent backgrounds or those who were born with a silver spoon. They are people who have learnt to embrace challenges, learn from them and give life their best shot.

Success in life demands that we constantly look at the brighter side. We cannot achieve much by wallowing in our shortcomings, misfortunes and the sad state of affairs. If we are going to experience true victory, we must arise from unnecessary pessimism, laziness and regressive thinking and purpose that we are going to change our circumstances for the better.

I concur with the author of this book when she refuses to be defined by the events that brought her to the lowest moments in her life. Indeed, she made lemonade out of the many lemons life threw at her. And that can be your story too.

Hon. Martha Karua
Member of Parliament - Gichugu Constituency.

ENDORSEMENT

*I*N THIS BOOK, broken to be made whole, you will learn many invaluable lessons of life. Winnie writes authentically for us to read and understand that tough times do not last, but tough people do.

This book shows that life has ups and downs. It will change your thinking and your life. A number of books lose touch with reality and the challenges that come as a result of living, not to mention attacks that come upon us from the enemy.

Winnie is gentle but gutsy. *Broken To Be Made Whole* is rooted in her faith in God. It will encourage you and offer a helping hand to pull you through whatever challenge you might face.

Listen to a woman who has been there; she comes from the high mountain of expectations to losing a child. She has learnt powerful lessons that she so generously shares in this book.

Winnie exhorts you to rise above the challenges; learn from life; build upon your blessings; continually make adjustments so that you are always on track to serve your highest purpose.

Thank you Winnie, for lifting people up and inspiring them for life's journey.

Pastor David Muriithi
Founder & Senior Pastor
House Of Grace Church - Nairobi.

BROKEN
TO BE MADE
Whole

A journey of loss, pain,
brokenness & restoration

WINNIE THUKU

Broken To Be Made Whole

ISBN: 9966153608

Copyright © 2010 By Winnie Thuku

P.O. Box 3875-00506

Nairobi, Kenya

Mobile: +254 722 425 618

Email: winnie.thuku@gmail.com

Publishing Consultants:
Aura Publishers

AURA BOOKS

Contents

Foreword .... *vii*

1. My Dance With Death 9
2. My Vote Of Confidence in God 25
3. A Season of Loneliness 38
4. A Season Of Letting Go And Letting God 47
5. A Season Of Being Still & Knowing That He Is God .. 59
6. My Extremity - My Wilderness - Became God's
   Opportunity 69
7. A Thorn Of His Planting? 76
8. Re-Digging My Wells 96
9. A Journey Of Self Forgiveness & The Resultant Joy .. 102
10. Learning To Acknowledge Him Before The Golden Bowl
    Is Broken 113
11. Another Loss And A Lesson In Giving 121
12. Being A Prophet Of My Own Life 132
13. Knowing That His Love Is Certain Even In Uncertain
    Circumstances 142
14. Experiencing His Sufficient Grace 152
15. Praising My Way To His Presence 158
16. Claiming His Power-filled Promises 169
17. Learning To Call Him Jehovah Shalom: The Lord My
    Peace 178
18. Learning To Call Him Jehovah Rophe (Rapha): The Lord
    My Healer 187
19. Learning To Call Him Jehovah Nissi: The Lord My
    Banner 192
20. Learning To Appreciate The Wonder Of Creation .. 197
21. Destiny Now Beckons 202

ACKNOWLEDGEMENTS

I acknowledge my Lord and Saviour, Jesus Christ who has been, still is and will remain my all in all. My strength, my joy, my refuge, my present help in times of need, my deliverer, the rock of my salvation, the darling of my heart, and the lover of my soul

I thank my family & friends, for standing in the gap for me when I needed them most. You have been a pillar of support, and a source of encouragement. Your support, whether spiritual, emotional, physical or material, means a lot to me.

I thank my spiritual authority, Bishop Allan Kiuna & Pastor Kathy Kiuna, for being the best that there can be. It is an honour to be under your covering.

I also appreciate Bishop David Mureithi. I thank God for your encouragement and your kind words.

And now to a lady that I look up to, a true leader, patriot, a woman of integrity, and courage! I appreciate you Honourable Martha Karua.

Last but not least, I thank my supportive friends, those who liked my writing from the word go and encouraged me on. Your positive feedback kept me writing more and more. It gave me motivation to know that my articles were encouraging someone out there.

For there is hope for a tree, If it is cut down, that it will sprout again, and that its tender shoots will not cease.

Job 14:7

FOREWORD

*H*EARTACHE AND PAIN come to almost everyone in life. However, not many people are able to go through what the author has gone through and turn it to their advantage. This is truly a story of pain, loss and then victory over the very things that threatened to take her down.

Having being raised in a family where she was not accepted, Winnie grew up an angry girl and although everything looked normal to any onlooker, the part in her that really mattered was wounded and full of pus that only her Maker could deal with. Winnie plots in clear and elaborate terms how the simmering bitterness and hopelessness was turned around.

A streak of light started to shine upon her life when she conceived her baby and she began to hope again. This baby, though not yet born was what Winnie lived for and dreamt of - a perfect life with her "angel." However it was not meant to be and the streak of light soon turn to gloom and depression. When her expectation was almost becoming a reality, the unexpected happened and she lost her baby in a near death experience and this became her point of inception into a journey that would take her through a path of pain, loneliness and betrayal by the very person that should have understood her the most. It is in this period that she renewed her commitment to Christ and learnt to forgive others and depend on Him for strength. She refused to wallow in self-pity and bitterness and decided to take control of her life.

In this book, Winnie chronicles her experiences and imparts the principles that helped her turn her discouragement into courage to tread on her hurts. She points out key principle such as praise, thanksgiving and service to others who were also in pain. She thus got her healing as she was able to be of service to those who were hurting.

I recommend this book to all who have gone through issues that left them with a wounded spirit and a hatred for life. The grace of God upon the author for the healing of those who are wounded is evident. Perhaps most conspicuous is the spirit in which she writes. There is no trace of the former bitterness, a clear indication that she was able to forgive and release those who had caused her so much pain. The difference between a scar and a wound is that when you press the latter there is still pain. Winnie has more than touched her scars and the pain is gone, showing that though she was broken, she has been made whole.

Bishop Allan Kiuna
Founder & General Overseer
Jubilee Christian Church

Chapter 1

My Dance With Death

The Sunshine

*T*HE NOISE IN the *matatu* was way too loud. My day had been busy and all I wanted was some peace and quiet. Unfortunately I did not have the luxury of choosing what type of *matatu* to board since it was rush hour and I needed to get home in a hurry. You see, I had just received some very bad news. I had been trying to get pregnant, but every month I kept getting my periods and was starting to get worried.

I had wanted to get pregnant ever since I finished college but I was just never ready financially because I wanted my baby to have the best. Then I was ready, but my body refused to cooperate. I knew it was not yet menopause so I kept trying. I had just visited a clinic in town, got tested and it was official, all my nocturnal efforts had been in vain, I was not pregnant!

Nonetheless, I had been feeling very weird, getting sickly every now and then and feeling tired in the mornings. I had a helpless feeling that some other force was in control of my body. The sicker I got however, the happier I became, because it could only mean one thing - that I was pregnant. Thus, the news from the clinic that I had not yet conceived was a big blow. In my heart of hearts, I refused to believe the results.

When I alighted from the *matatu** at our local shopping centre, I saw a million signboards, but the only one that struck my eye was the chemist. Why believe the clinic's results when I can always do my own test at home? So straight to the chemist I rushed, bought a pregnancy test kit and literally ran home. After about five minutes, I was dancing around my house like a chicken on crack. Yes, I was pregnant!

The rest as they say is history. Morning sickness, noontime sickness, evening sickness, night sickness, all day sickness... I had this never-ending fatigue, weird cravings, swollen belly,

*matatu - minibus

face and legs and all the symptoms that come with pregnancy. Sometimes it was painful but mostly lovely since I knew I was helping God in His grand plan of creation, mmh...partnership with the Almighty!

The excitement was too much. Just at one month I could already figure myself wearing the cute maternity dresses, I already had images of me rocking her in my arms. I dreamt of the relationship we would have, how we would laugh together, how we would cry together. Stupid as it may sound, I could even imagine her crying for my attention. I was already being careful with what I ate because I did not want to put my baby at risk. I even started journalizing my thoughts and actions as every minute was precious.

* * * * * * * * * * * * * * * * * * * *

It's been a rocky ride, but a ride worth taking nonetheless. So today I am just 4 weeks away from my EDD, Expected Date of Delivery. It's a Saturday afternoon and I want to do some last minute shopping for *toto**. Today I will not go home with our company driver as it is the norm. My cousin is with me and we want some privacy so we opt to take a *matatu** home. There is a hill between the bus stage and my house. Walking down the hill, I hold my tummy as if it's contents are going to spill out anytime. There is certain heaviness just below my tummy. I tell myself that it is normal.

The Pain, The Loss, and The Bad Report

We are having an exciting evening, and since I haven't been to our village in a long time, some old time gossip keeps my clock ticking. Soon it is bedtime. I need some sleep but my toto won't let me - she is always playing and kicking when I need to sleep. At around midnight I feel like going for a long call I lazily stroll towards the bathroom. The urge is so much but surprisingly when I get ready to do my potty business, there is nothing, completely nothing, save for an enormous release of gas.

I go back to bed, and in the next one hour I have visited the bathroom more than 10 times, and still nothing. I am a first time mom so I have no clue what is going on. My cousin is a mom already, but I think she is too sleepy to think straight. It is only when I start getting sharp back pains that she suggests that I could be in labour.

I am scared from all the stories I have heard about child birth. I call my doctor when the pain gets worse and he explains that it could be false labour. He advises that I give myself some time to see if it goes away. But this is not the kind of pain that could be termed as false labour. My whole body is about to explode. The pain gets worse: pain, pain, and more pain! A pain so agonizing - actually worse than anything I have experienced before. My doctor advises me to rush to the nearest hospital for a check just in case it is not false labour.

My trip to the hospital is very short but one that will forever stick in my mind. In my state of pain and agony, I do unimaginable things, including undressing in the car and calling the taxi driver all sorts of names. Right now, I want to convince myself that am just having stomach cramps because my baby isn't due yet. But no! These must be the contractions they talk about because right now my body is engulfed in excruciating pain..

In less than ten minutes, I find myself at the hospital reception waiting to be booked in. It is a chilly Sunday morning, the day I will never forget. As soon as I am booked in, a nurse comes to attend to me. I am now screaming at the top of my voice; the pain is just unbearable. She walks out for about five minutes and then another nurse walks in. She asks me to lie on my left side then asks me to describe how am feeling. I tell her that it's like my tummy is moving to one side. She then tells me to lie on my right side, and the same thing happens. She walks out.

She then returns and gives me an injection which am made to understand will ease my pain. She comments that my palms and eyes are paper white then walks out. All this time, my family is gathered outside my room and no one is allowed in. My mom comes in after several minutes, I ask her what is going on and she tells me that everything is okay, am just in labour. Yeah, just in labour! So this is what women in labour go through? A pain that increases in tempo until you feel like you are in another world, like you are going out of your mind? A pain so unbearable and terrifying you feel like every part of your body is being ripped apart?

After the injection the pain eases a little then returns after some time, this time even more intense. What I don't know is that all this time, the doctors are organizing for a blood transfusion because apparently I am short of blood. I don't understand. I haven't even shed a drop of blood and am already short of blood? After a few hours I am put on the drip for induced labour. I am now in excruciating pain. I then ask the nurse if everything is okay. What she says rings so painfully in my mind even today, "Right now you are our priority, not your baby. It's your life we are trying to save".

"What do you mean? My baby means everything to me and now you tell me she is not a priority? Does that mean what I'm thinking? That my baby is dead?"

I now scream at the top of my voice calling out to my mum. I ask her to tell me the truth. I see the sad look in her eyes and I know she knows. She tells me something like I will be okay.

Just then a doctor walks in and asks me to try and remember my movements over the past few days. I ask Why?

It is then that the doctors start explaining that my baby suffocated in my womb and died a few hours ago.

I don't know if there is any explanation that can comfort me. I painfully tell the doctor how a week ago I slid while adjusting my window curtain. I did not fall down because I held on to my bed. My baby had stopped playing for a few minutes then started again. Still, I had called my doctor who had explained that if I was not bleeding then I was okay, but still advised that I go for a scan the following morning.

The scan confirmed that my baby was OK and that I was out of danger. What we didn't know was that the impact was too small to be detected at that time. Apparently the placenta had dislodged from the uterus, a distance so tiny that not even a scan could detect. With time, the placenta had slowly disconnected from the uterus, until last night, when it fully dislodged, cutting off my baby's supply of oxygen.

Right now my body is still in a lot of pain, but the emotional pain seems to overshadow the physical pain. Everything is now in a haze. All my hopes are cruelly cut short. The despair and pain that I now feel is horrendous. I feel inadequate for not carrying my baby to full term.

But the battle is just beginning. My blood pressure shoots up as soon as I learn about my baby. This now makes my condition even worse because according to the doctors, the reason I have very little blood is that I have been bleeding internally for a whole week and now my system is almost running out of blood. Although transfusion is now ongoing, the doctors confirm that am losing more blood than am gaining.

My mother now makes calls to other family members and friends asking them to come and donate blood. Though my body has totally refused to respond to the drip, the doctors try their level best to make sure that I deliver the baby normally now that I cannot have a C-Section delivery with my BP so high.

For close to 3 painful days, the doctors keep hoping that my body will give way, there was no dilation even after all those injections and other medicines. For close to three eternal days, I painfully try to push an already dead baby. In those three painful days, I spend my last moments with my baby, knowing fully well that she will be too dead to smile back at me when she comes out, knowing that I will never hear her cry.

Things are now getting thick. My blood is now running out despite the fact that it is being transfused through both hands, and my body hasn't responded at all to any of their medical tricks. There are two options for me, both of which are now fatal. The first is to continue waiting to give birth normally and risk bleeding to death. The second is to have a Caesarean section operation, but due to the high BP, still risk bleeding to death. It is a typical catch 22 situation; whichever option I take, the doctors explain that my chances of survival are almost nil!

By now my family and friends are traumatized. The physical pain is now so much that I don't really care about any consequences of my decision. All I want is to get my baby out - the fastest way possible. At this point I feel that I have reached my threshold of tolerance. I feel like the pangs of death are upon me. So I sign the papers. I am quickly wheeled into theatre where I am sedated within less than two minutes.

When I awake, I remember the first words I utter are "I am freezing!". It's then that I hear a lot of movement in the room. I don't know where I am, or what is happening, all I know is that I am almost freezing to death. I then ask the doctor why I am freezing. He thinks that I am aware of what just happened to me, so he tries to explain that I don't have enough blood to keep me warm. I still don't understand what he is talking about, but anyhow, he fetches a heater and heats up my room.

I am half asleep and half awake. I don't fully comprehend what is happening around me. One minute I know my baby is dead, the next minute I have forgotten and I start asking how my baby is doing. It is a total blur, like going through a haze, not knowing where I am coming from or where I am going.

I am now receiving very many visitors at the hospital, most of whom I do not know. But there is one particular lady I will never forget. It is a sunny morning and I wake up to find her consolingly rubbing my hand. She is not in a nurse uniform, and trying to recall, she doesn't look like any of my friends. So I ask who she is. She goes ahead to explain that she works at the hospital, in the accounts department. So what is she doing here? She explains that she had to come and witness the 'hospital's miracle'. And how so, I wonder. She then explains how all the hospital staff had been forced to donate blood although according to how the doctors were talking, I wasn't going to survive.

It is now that I begin to remember past events and understand just how serious my case was. Then minutes later another lady walks in. She introduces herself as part of the surgical team that operated on me. She calls me a 'Jesus girl'. She explains that my case was completely beyond the capability of the best doctors the world could produce. That they had done their part and waited for God to do His part. She goes on to tell me how they completely removed my uterus because it was badly damaged, and most of the surgeons were suggesting that they discard it, after all I was not expected to survive the surgery. She narrates that a few surgeons mentioned that just in case I survived, I could sue the hospital for removing my uterus without my approval. Plus they had no right to play God, and that is how I got to keep my uterus.

It is when this lady is giving me all this account that my mum walks in, and at this point she gathers the guts to tell me just how serious the case was. She tells me that one particular doctor had openly told her that the reason they were taking me to theatre was so that my baby and I could be buried separately. Then I woke up much to the shock of everyone. I woke up and proved to the world that my work on earth is not yet done. I woke up and proved that there is a God whose miracles defy all medical reasoning. While science postulated that I was not going to survive the surgery, God on the other hand declared that everything is possible with Him, and He affirmed that He changes not, that He is the same yesterday, today and forever (Hebrews 13:8).

* * * * * * * * * * * * * * * * * * * *

Whose Report Will You Believe?

That was a season when Ron Kenoly's song constantly rang in my mind, "Whose report will you believe? We shall believe the report of the Lord." Seeing that doctors had written me off because I was losing more blood than I was gaining, seeing that doctors completely believed that I would not survive the operation, all this made me wonder whether to believe their report or not. During the operation, the surgeons removed my uterus and wanted to throw it away before sewing my tummy back. Of course they did not think I would wake up from the operation so it really did not matter if I was buried with or without a uterus. But I thank God for one woman of faith, a female surgeon who told them to stop playing God. They hastily returned the uterus and sewed back my tummy. I am grateful for that woman of God who chose to exalt the report of the Lord over the report of her fellow surgeons. Were it not for her, today I would be without a uterus!

Isaiah 53:1-5 - "Who hath believed our report? And to whom is the arm of the Lord revealed? For He shall grow up before Him as a tender plant, and as a root out of a dry ground: He hath

17

no form nor comeliness; and when we shall see Him, there is no beauty that we should desire Him. He is despised and rejected of men; a man of sorrows, and acquainted with grief: and we hid as it were our faces from Him; He was despised, and we esteemed Him not. Surely He hath borne our griefs, and carried our sorrows: yet we did esteem Him stricken, smitten of God, and afflicted. But He was wounded for our transgressions, He was bruised for our iniquities: the chastisement of our peace was upon Him; and with His stripes we are healed."

That was a season when I learnt that our God still performs miracles even today, and even in a much greater dimension. Although the laws and verdicts of science have gained so much ground that almost everyone today exalts the words of science above the Word of God, I still chose to believe the report of the Lord. John 11:40 tells us that if we can believe, we can see the glory of the Lord. Mark 9: 23 goes on to tell us that everything is possible if we believe.

Maybe you have received a bad report from the doctors. Maybe they have told you that you will not be able to give birth because of some abnormalities. Maybe you are a man and the doctor has told you that you cannot father a child because your sperm count is too low, or maybe they have told you that you have cancer and you only have a few months to live. Maybe they have told you that you are suffering from a disease whose name you cannot even pronounce (you know those names that doctors give to diseases that they can't handle?). Well, if they have given you the diagnosis, do not dwell to much on it. Instead, try and look for a *Rapha* word from God that will no doubt turn around your situation.

Today place a demand in heaven for your good report that will counter the doctors bad report. *"Whatsoever things are true, whatsoever things are just, whatsoever things are pure, whatsoever things are of good report, if there be any virtue, and if there be any praise, think of these things"* (Philippians 4:8).

I am not trying to downplay the validity of these scientific reports. All I want you to know is that there is a God in heaven who specializes in what man deems impossible, and He is the supreme arbiter, more than able to heal you. Scientific reports will no doubt give you facts, but God's word will give you the truth! And the truth shall set you free from your bondage of sickness. Just believe! What His mouth has promised, His hand will perform and He is not a man that He should lie, He will not change His mind! Don't rely so much on your five senses; rely on the one who gave you the five senses.

Against all hope, Sarah believed in God that she would one day have a child. If she was living in today's world, doctors would have termed her case as just impossible. They would not even have wasted their time thinking about her case. She was way past menopause and there is no way science would have given her a good report. Her case was unfixable! But God being God, He proved to everyone that what water is to a hopeless tree is what His Word is to a hopeless situation. He gave Sarah a baby boy in her old age! This is a formidable reinforcement of what the bible says in Job 14:7, that there is hope for a tree even if it is cut down, for it will sprout again, and its new shoots will not fail.

Remember the woman who had the issue of blood. She had stayed for many years with her sickness and no doctor or expert was able to give her a good report for her case. However, it only took a touch of Jesus' cloak. What faith! A faith based on the belief that the doctors did not have the last word. Her faith was based on the belief that God - rather than medical facts - held the last word regarding her case. The bible says that her bleeding stopped immediately and she felt in her body that she was freed from her suffering.

If God is voting in favour of your healing today, why not appreciate it by stretching your faith towards Jesus the same way that woman did, and touch the hem of His garment?

From the day of my surgery, since they removed my uterus and returned it, I have done two ultra sound tests and the doctors tell me that my uterus shows no signs of ever having being removed. In fact, it is so intact that they don't believe it when I tell them that the uterus was returned in a hurry because I was losing blood and they needed to sew me back quickly. They don't believe it when I tell them that the surgeons did not even put it back in its rightful place - that they just threw it back in. Romans 4:17 says that He is the God who gives life to the dead, and calls things that are not as though they are! I am so privileged to be a living testimony to that word. And my testimony is not over yet, I believe that some day very soon, I am going to be a mother, claiming what Exodus 23: 25 – 26 says, that He shall take away sickness from among us, and none shall miscarry or be barren in our land, and that He shall give us a full life span.

So today, when doctors pronounce your case as hopeless, when they tell you that your case is impossible, that it has never been done before and it cannot be done now, whose report will you believe? The experts' report or the report of the one who says in Jeremiah 32:27 that He is the Lord, the God of all mankind, and that nothing is too hard for Him? Even the bible warns us in 1Timothy 6:20-21 to guard what has been entrusted to our care, to turn away from godless chatter and the opposing ideas of what is falsely called knowledge, with which some have professed and in so doing have wondered from the faith.

Believe the Lord today to tickle the ears of they that will hear of your miracle, and to amaze the eyes of those who will see your miracle happen right before their eyes. Believe God to bring about healing and physical restoration to your body and cause people to behold His power through your miracle today. Hezekiah of old was once told that he only had a few days to live, but he ended up living for over a decade more. That God of Hezekiah is still God today.

I need someone to help me preach this gospel of a God of impossibilities. This gospel states that once a situation has been certified as impossible in the natural, it has just opened a way for the supernatural to take over. If you know someone who has been written off by doctors, allow me to charge you to take this gospel of our God who specializes in the impossibilities of doctors and experts, I charge you to encourage them that there is hope even after a tree has been cut down. I charge you to lay hands on the sick just as the bible has commanded.

Mark 16: 17-18 assures that signs and wonders shall follow those who believe Him. If He proved the doctors and experts wrong in my case, He can do it for you too! All you have to do is invoke the supernatural into your case.

Healing And Comfort

My heart is still feeble as I try to explain what I have been going through since I lost my baby. The healing process has been painful both physically and emotionally. I walk around sometimes trying to smile, trying to make everyone think that I am okay, but there is this wave of sadness that sometimes overwhelms me, knowing just how much I miss my baby girl.

Beneath all my tears, all my pain, my hurt, my anger and all the turmoil, there is however an abiding peace that comes from God. It is a peace that tells me that God will never leave me nor forsake me and it comes from knowing that one day I will understand why my baby had to leave me before I even held her in my arms. I don't understand anything right now, but I trust in God and I know that even though I am hard pressed on every side, I am not crushed; even though I am struck down, I am not destroyed.

A few months after losing my baby I lost one of my friends. She passed away a few minutes after waking up from a Caesarian section operation - after developing high blood pressure during the operation. Her baby boy survived but she never lived to hold him in her arms. So I know that I am very blessed to have woken up from that operation room and lived to tell my story. I have so many questions for which I will probably never get the answers. However, I know that God is faithful no matter what I am going through.

I now write this story sobbing, feeling so lonely at times especially when I have to rekindle memories so as to tell you my story. A few years back I was the happiest person on earth. My baby's tiny kicks kept me up at night and it was awesome. There have been days when I have cried myself to sleep, wondering how it could be today if she had survived. There have been times when I woke up in the middle of the night just needing someone to tell me that it was just a dream, only to realize that this was now my new reality. There have been nights when I cried and asked God to take me and let me be with my baby. Nonetheless, with tears streaming down my face, I am very thankful that I am alive to tell everyone that I dined with death, I had my dance with death, I wrestled with death, but I conquered!

As always, God knew how to comfort me. So far He has not left me comfortless. In His own divine way He has taught me once again how to make melodies, He has once again taught my heart how to be glad. He has given me beauty for ashes. He has replaced my emancipated mourning face, burnt from my scalding tears with a radiant beautiful face. He has so far replaced the redness in my eyes with a sparkle. His grace has shone on my face, giving me a visible beauty, and a gracious and unfading loveliness. I may have gone through a night of mourning and grief, but He has made my morning to sparkle with dew, a morning full of His joy. Oh He has given me a garment of praise for a spirit of heaviness. He has also drawn me closer to Himself and made me a tree of righteousness, a tree of His own planting, that He might be glorified through me!

As you continue reading this book, as I narrate my grieving experience and tell you just how losing my baby evoked a string of other unfortunate happenings, and how all these have brought me closer to my God, and as you see how God through this experience has taught me that my path back to faithfulness lay in going through a season of brokenness before Him, just remember that I sought to know the intentions of God for my suffering, my loss, my emptiness, for I knew there was going to be glory in my storm.

As strange (and selfish to my baby) as it may sound, and for very many reasons, am glad that I passed through the trauma of losing my baby. Somewhat, through her loss, my life has gained and i have passed through lessons that have been so valuable to me. Two years ago I would not have said this, but it is now that the pieces of the puzzles fit together. But do not mistake me; even though she was here for just a short while, she still had a purpose in this life, no matter how short-lived. It is my prayer that my story, my loss and my pain will not be in vain. I wish to encourage someone today. The same way my experience has served to enrich my life, I pray it will enrich your life as you read this book.

I wish to encourage someone who might be going through a stormy situation, not from the perspective of an expert but from the perspective of one who has gone through it, and conquered. We may not necessarily be at the same point in our growth process, so your story might not be identical to mine. The path that the Lord took with me might not be the same as yours. There may be things in this books you will not wholly agree with. Well it is just my story. Wisely pick what will minister to you and move towards your healing in Jesus name. Go on, blossom out of your dark valley like I did, because yes, I dined with death, I danced with death, I wrestled with death, but I conquered! And you too can!

SCRIPTURE FOCUS

Psalm 23
The Lord is my shepherd;
I shall not want.
He makes me to lie down in green pastures;
He leads me beside the still waters.
He restores my soul;
He leads me in the paths of righteousness
For His name's sake.
Yea, though I walk
through the valley of the shadow of death,
I will fear no evil; For You are with me;
Your rod and Your staff, they comfort me.
You prepare a table before me
in the presence of my enemies;
You anoint my head with oil;
My cup runs over.
Surely goodness and mercy
shall follow me All the days of my life;
And I will dwell in the house of the Lord Forever.

Chapter 2

My Vote Of Confidence In God

You are my sunshine, my only sunshine,
You make me happy when skies are grey,
You never know dear how much I love you,
Please don't take my sunshine away.

*T*HESE ARE THE words of a song that I sang subconsciously some times back. I had bonded with my little sunshine so much that I would never have imagined my life without her. Then came the storm, and my sunshine passed on. A few hours prior, everything had seemed perfect. It seemed quite impossible that the beautiful blue skies up high could be replaced in a flash of a moment by dark clouds hovering over my life, signalling the ultimate start of the battle between good and evil. It was evident that I was now in a big storm.

So how does one walk through such a storm? When God gives you a gift and then takes it away from you, is there any more reason for living? Is there any hope for the future? The bible says that blessed is the fruit of your womb, but what happens when this blessing is cruelly snatched away from you? What happened? Did I somehow slip out of His care for a moment? Did God somehow abandon me for a split second? Why was I left to continue living when my baby girl was not even given a chance to see the sun? Why should I try to go on living when my whole world has been totally shattered and shaken to its foundation? Why bother picking up the pieces? How could I go on when the very fabric of my existence had been torn apart and all that I had left was unending sorrow and total shock?

These were some of the many questions I recycled over my mind. As the questions continued to echo and no answers were forthcoming, anger began to build in me and I grew more frustrated.

The fact that my baby girl died before birth did not make things any better. No one seemed to understand the kind of pain I was going through. For most people, I simply had a miscarriage; for others, it was a still birth; but only a few felt the pain of losing my baby, not as a foetus, but as a baby that I felt kick inside me for more than eight months. I longed that one day I would hold, kiss and rock my baby to sleep and love her for many years. Not only had I lost a child, but I also lost hope and confidence. It was hard looking at the baby's clothes, and all the other baby stuff that I had already bought anticipating her. It was even harder when people (who were not aware of my loss) called me to ask when I was due, or how the baby was. It is painful enough that there is no grave I can visit since burials from still births are done by the hospital. It is hard to look at birth and death certificates that have no names.

The grief that I was going through was like a forest fire that could not be contained, or one that could not have been prevented. It came at a time when I least expected it, and just as a fire consumes a forest, so was the grief consuming to my soul. I hurt so much until I felt that there could never be a bigger form of pain in life. I felt that my life had been reduced to one big heap of ashes. Only charred remains of hope and dreams were left for me to see. All that I had anticipated remained a far away dream and a distant fantasy. In my heart I tried to remember the beautiful memories of my baby kicking. I tried to focus on the happy times I had with her, but in my mind I only saw devastation.

I wondered if there was ever going to be any hope in my life again. My heart had been broken into a million pieces, and I was convinced that no one in the whole world could understand what I was going through. I kept smiling at people, but on the inside my pain was too deep for me to find comfort from anyone. Many are the times I would be talking happily with my friends and family, and then suddenly tears would flow freely down my cheeks and my countenance would just drop, often to the amazement of those in my company. I needed Jesus since I couldn't take the pain anymore.

Mark 4:35-41 tells of a stormy situation that Jesus had with His disciples at the sea. They were afraid and fearful for their lives. They tried to do everything they could but there seemed to be no headway, so they turned to Jesus who was asleep. Jesus' response to the situation was a perfect display of His power over circumstances. With a little whisper He stilled the storm and quieted the waves of the sea. The disciples had not yet known who Jesus really was and we see them asking each other "...Who is this? Even the wind and the waves obey Him!" This was a perfect display of the Divine person in Him.

What keeps us strong in a storm is our knowledge of Jesus, His promises and who He is in our lives. It is the knowledge of His power, His character, the fact that He is God and that He has plans to give us hope and a future. We need constantly to know that our names are engraved on the palms of His hands and that "...He will command His angels concerning you to guard you in all your ways, they (the angels) will lift you up in their hands so that you will not strike your foot against a stone..." Psalms 91:11-12. Also key is our knowledge of who God says we are. If He says that we are blessed, then we are blessed, if He says that we are healed, then we are healed. This knowledge leaves no room for doubt or negotiations even though the devil may try the hardest to feed us with feelings of remorse, guilt, extreme sadness, and even condemnation.

In Matthew 14:29, we read the story of Peter when he saw Jesus walking on the water. When Jesus told him to go to Him, Peter panicked. He started to see the waves instead of seeing the master of the waves. He started paying attention to the waves instead of looking unto Him who had called him. That is when he began to sink. Then Jesus reached out His hand to Peter and that is when Peter's fears disappeared and he gained his balance and finally walked on the water, just like Jesus. Even today, Jesus wants us to take our eyes off our circumstances. He wants us to cast off our fears and look upon Him, obey Him when He calls us.

Life as it is today is full of heartaches. There is so much misery in the world. Every time you turn on the television, you are saddened by the suffering of humankind. Although God did not promise us sunshine throughout, we rejoice in knowing that He will be with us every step of the way, and each step will be a miracle. We can rely on Him to renew our strength day by day, and make all crooked paths straights. Sometimes we do not have the strength to face another day, but if God has loved us enough to grant us another day, then all we have to do is show up, be present, and let His miracles unfold. The same way He came through for the disciples in the face of their disaster, on the face of the deep, is the same way He will come through for you in your storm.

Without this knowledge of who God is in our lives, we might be overcome by fear, cowardice and timidity. By this we basically are portraying a vote of no confidence in our God. Many are the times when we are put to extreme pressure, but we have to keep our faith and look up to the promising God who says that He will never leave us nor forsake us. This is the promise that faith clings to when we are hard hit. True peace can only come from this kind of faith in Him, because only His hand, the hand that made the tears, can reach deep down to its sources and dry them up.

I am constantly reminded of the love He has for me, an unconditional love that is like a river that flows freely, abundantly and never runs dry. The love He has for me cannot be broken by anyone or any circumstances. He loves me not because I deserve it but simply because He has chosen to love me, with all my faults, failures, problems and weaknesses. It is this knowledge of the deep love He has for me that makes me strong in times of storms. Sometimes I feel so alone without my baby; I feel completely empty, but I have learnt to approach the Lord for a refill, and God has sure opened continuous channels of His love to me. I have continued to have a bountiful immeasurable store of love.

Maybe you are looking around and all you see is a darkness so thick you cannot make head or tail of your situation. Maybe you do not see where you have come from or where you are headed. Maybe you are doubting what His word says in Psalms 139:11-12, that the darkness shall surely not cover you. You are doubting if it is true that even the darkest hour shall not hide His face from you. The message that the Lord has for you this day is not that the darkness is not thick, and the storm is not fierce; His message is that despite these glaring threats, He is greater than the storm!

Psalms 30:5 - ". . . weeping may endure for a night, but joy comes in the morning."

Maybe you have wept for so long that your experience only seems to demonstrate the falsity of this verse. Maybe it has reached a point where you think that this verse is just but a piece of beautiful poetry with no serious truth in it. Maybe you think the psalmist stubbornly refused to accept the ugly facts of life, and even shut his eyes to the everyday tragedies of life that bring with them tears that last for a long time. On the contrary, the psalmist only faced these terrifying calamities but chose to cling to his faith. Just like the psalmist, I chose to believe that even though tears may come in the night, they will surely vanish with the rising of the sun, just like the morning dew. I know that He will turn my mourning into dancing, and it is this hope that enables me to see things through when all else is gone.

My knowledge of who my God is in my life gives me a hope that lights up in my darkest hour, a hope that plucks sorrow's bitterest sting. For as long as I believe that joy comes in the morning, no matter what storm comes my way, my heart will never be completely downcast. When my sunshine faded, I even asked God whether He could not resurrect her, I just wanted my baby girl back, and I knew the God of today is still the God who called Lazarus from the dead.

But even when God did not answer my prayers, I knew that He was doing something in me that was vastly better than my request, He was giving me an inner strength and a courage that would enable me to bear it all. He gave me a confidence in Him that made me say that in the presence of pain and even in the face of death itself, His joy would come to me in its fullness.

Today I look back and see the finer and fuller sense of God's reassurance to me that my sorrow shall be turned into joy, and today, looking how far God has brought me, I cannot help but mock death, *"Death, oh death, where is thy sting?"*

Coming to terms with my baby's death was so difficult but the Lord continually reminded me that she was now safe in the care of His loving arms. He kept reminding me that she had gone to new horizons, brighter days, so I had not lost her. I knew that even though I could not see her, or hear her cry, or rub her cheek against mine, or kiss her tiny mouth, I knew that this is just a time of distance between us. I found and still find hope in knowing that God does all things in love, and He did not take her away from me to hurt me, or crush or break me the way the devil wanted me broken. I find strength in knowing that God is protecting her, loving her, and she is safe and happy, just waiting for me, and I know that one day I shall be able to hold her in my arms, kiss her and tell her all the stories that I never got to tell her.

It is just a matter of time and I shall soon see her all happy, bright and shinning. She now represents me in the kingdom, maybe she is a little cherub, I don't know, but every time I feel alone, it gives me much encouragement to know where she is. I no longer weep over her. I no longer waste time lamenting and complaining over her loss. I stopped blaming myself for not carrying her to full term. I no longer let my heart be troubled.

At the time of writing this book, it has now been two years, and over this time, I have come to realize that even though the ashes from that experience could never have been washed away in my tears, I am now alive again. These ashes revitalized me and brought forth new life in me, just like the natural rain soaks in the ashes and uses these ashes to revitalize the soil so that new life may begin. Even though my tears never washed away my pain, they regenerated my broken spirit and started a new growth in me, one shoot at a time. My world may have fallen apart but I now see beauty in place of the ashes.

It has taken time to heal but in every step of the way, I continue to lean on God and rely on His comfort and His strength knowing full well that what He is giving me is beauty for ashes. I now continue to hang on to that hope that one day I shall see my baby girl in heaven.

After having gone through all that, and after asking all the endless questions, I now have come to accept just one answer to all those questions, and the answer is that only God knows! You can try to give me any other answers; you could try to second-guess God, but dare you not, because you do not have His wisdom, or His knowledge and it would only be foolish of you to do so. You do not need to know a lot of things, all you need to do is trust Him and give Him your vote of confidence. He knows why, the same way He knows why He created day and night; the same way He knows why He created the moon, the sun, the stars and placed them in their exact locations. His ways are higher than our ways, His thoughts are higher than our thoughts.

God knows why you had to go through a certain calamity the same way He knows why He created you. Sometimes the hardest thing to do is to give Him your vote of confidence, but that is all He wants us to do. The pain and heartache are for real, but His love for you is real too, and is deeper than you could ever imagine. He is the one who will lift your head up when you feel like you cannot face tomorrow. He is the one who will direct your feet even when you move one foot in front not knowing exactly where to move it.

Psalms 91:1 - "He that dwelleth in the secret place of the most high shall abide under the shadow of the Almighty."

Joblessness is a monstrous wave that is rocking the lives of our youth. Our young men and women are beaten, bruised and battered, and with nowhere to turn to, they wonder if they can survive the storm. To you who is going through a season of joblessness, God wants you to know that even when that prospective employer keeps promising to call you back, and it now seems like He will never, keep your eyes on the Lord, for He is the one who will make a way for you.

For now, decide to soar high above the storms just like an eagle does and do not let the burdens of this life weigh you down. As you do that, the Lord has promised that He shall renew your strength and you therefore shall not grow weary. He is a God of justice and He will be gracious to you and show you His compassion, in His own time. Keep reminding God of His promise to you that whenever you call Him, He shall come to your rescue. Keep praising Him because He is in the battlefield with you.

The Lord did not promise that there would be no pain; He only promised to give us strength, He only promised never to leave us, He only promised us that He shall be with us to the end of time. Remember the story of Simon Peter in the book of Luke 22: 31-32. Jesus knew that Simon Peter was going to face a big storm, but He did not promise him that He would take away the storm. Instead, He promised that He had prayed for him. *"Simon, Simon, Satan has asked to sift you as wheat. But I have prayed for you, Simon, that your faith may not fail. And when you have turned back, strengthen your brothers."*

These scriptures just make me put all my confidence in my God, knowing that no mater what storm comes my way, I am not alone, the Holy Spirit is making intercessions on my behalf. He will do the same for you so why don't you give Him your vote of confidence today?

As you face your storm today, remember to focus on the bigness of our God, and not the bigness of your storm. For sure, the steps to victory are usually moist with tears, but remember that the Lord knows your needs and He cares for you. He understands your weaknesses, He will strengthen your faith, He will be your harbour of safety in the storms of life, He will be a rock that you can cling on to. He tells us in Isaiah 43:2 that when we pass through the waters He will be with us, and when we pass through the rivers, they will not sweep over us. When we walk through the fire, we will not be burned, and the flames will not consume us. There are so many things that our finite minds do not know and cannot even begin to fathom. Maybe you get angry and wonder why God does not prevent bad things from happening to you, but choose to give Him your vote of confidence because He knows not just your past and present, but your future too.

True, not all situations will have a happy ending; not all tragedies will have a miraculous ending that we can all talk about, even for those people who have been faithful to the Lord. We hear of very bad, painful and traumatic things happening to good people. We hear of innocent children getting raped, we hear of fathers killing their families, we hear of men of God perishing in plane crashes, we hear of women of God dying of breast cancer, but our heavenly Father is still God and He is there even in the most painful of circumstances.

As you read this book, maybe you are in the midst of a storm that just wont go away but only seems to come back with more flashes of lightning and outbursts of thunder. Darkness seems to overpower the light and it feels like the storm may never end. Whatever storm you may face today, you can speak to it and still it down. Even though I do not know the kind of storm that is raging in your life, I am here to tell you that I know the one who walks on the waves. He will command peace to your storm. Likewise, I am constantly learning to speak into my situations, commanding peace and the will of God into my life. I am learning to have a child-like faith that focuses on the bigness of my God and not the bigness of my situation. I now live on Faith Street where I can move mountains. Even when I do not understand my situation, I still choose to believe in God and give Him a vote of confidence. I have learnt that the darkest moments of one's life may carry the seeds of the brightest future, and that the same storm am facing today is the same storm that carries an abundance of rain, an abundance of blessings.

SCRIPTURE FOCUS

Psalms 91

He who dwells in the secret place of the Most High Shall abide under the shadow of the Almighty.

I will say of the LORD, "He is my refuge and my fortress; My God, in Him I will trust."

Surely He shall deliver you from the snare of the fowler And from the perilous pestilence.

He shall cover you with His feathers, And under His wings you shall take refuge; His truth shall be your shield and buckler.

You shall not be afraid of the terror by night, Nor of the arrow that flies by day,

Nor of the pestilence that walks in darkness, Nor of the destruction that lays waste at noonday.

A thousand may fall at your side, And ten thousand at your right hand; But it shall not come near you.

Only with your eyes shall you look, And see the reward of the wicked.

Because you have made the LORD, who is my refuge, Even the Most High, your dwelling place,

No evil shall befall you, Nor shall any plague come near your dwelling;

For He shall give His angels charge over you, To keep you in all your ways.

In their hands they shall bear you up, Lest you dash your foot against a stone.

You shall tread upon the lion and the cobra, The young lion and the serpent you shall trample underfoot.

"Because he has set his love upon Me, therefore I will deliver him; I will set him on high, because he has known My name.

He shall call upon Me, and I will answer him; I will be with him in trouble; I will deliver him and honor him.

With long life I will satisfy him, And show him My salvation.".

Chapter 3

A Season of Loneliness

*"Lord, you seem so far away, a million miles or more it seems today.
And though I haven't lost my faith, I must confess right now;
that it's hard for me to pray. But I don't know what to say,
and I don't know where to start. But as you give the grace,
with all that's in my heart, I will sing,... Even in my darkest hour,
through the sorrow and the pain..." — Don Moen*

I KNOW JUST TOO well the kind of feeling singer and songwriter Don Moen had when he wrote this song.

Do you sometimes feel alone and abandoned? Do you go through life's hardships feeling as though nobody, not even God, cares? Does God seem completely distant, a million miles away when you need Him most? Well, you are not alone. Most of us go through seasons in life when we question whether God is really there; we question His very presence in our lives.

A few months after the loss of my baby, a time came when my family who were keeping me company started moving back to their homes one by one. My cousin left, then my mother (save for the occasional weekend visits). I became so overwhelmed with loneliness. I was in my world alone where I felt physically, emotionally and psychologically alienated. I was disconnected from the world. My days became an endless maze of boring meaningless routine of waking up, taking breakfast, sitting in front of the TV, making lunch, another session of watching TV, making supper, watching TV, and sleeping. The nights became worse as I even found it harder to sleep. I tried to spend time praying, singing, reading, but I had too much time at my disposal. I would wake up at night and rummage through my stuff from room to room, clean the rooms at night. It was just too much for me to bear.

It hurt so much to be so idle and alone when everyone else seemed very busy with their work and their lives. I tried to do everything in my power to avoid idleness but seemingly, whatever I did was just not enough. I tried to reach out to friends but most of them were too busy for me. I waited for my friends to call me but it reached a point where I would go a whole day without hearing my phone ring. At some point I even forgot the sound of my phone's ring tone. Many of my attempts to initiate conversations with friends failed miserably. Most of them assumed that I was calling to ask for a favour, yet all I wanted was someone to talk to.

The loneliness started taking a whole new turn as I started to become depressed. I would cry so much at times I wondered how I did not die of dehydration. I longed for the day I would get my peace of heart and mind again. But God is God, and He is good. Some of the people I never expected to stick by me surprised me the most by being there for me. Some of them were strangers who offered me tremendous support and were a constant source of strength. I saw myself establishing bonds of friendship and support with my new friends, even though I missed my old friends and wished that they were there for me. It was a time when I learned a lot about friendships.

It was when I was toying around with my laptop that an idea came to me, and I decided to jot down my feelings at that moment. I started writing letters to God, just telling him what I was feeling. I started writing down my prayers. At first I would write and then delete. All this was just an expression of the ongoing internal battles with the loss of my daughter even though in the eyes of everyone else she seemed gone.

Then one day my uncle sent me a copy of a local newspaper where he is a contributor. I was just supposed to read his article, but we ended up chatting and I jokingly told him I would like to contribute too. To cut the long story short, my writing career was birthed. My writing was birthed out of pain, and loneliness. I began to contribute articles on a weekly basis, mostly social, economical, political pieces, as well as devotional material that touched on what I was going through at that time. I quickly gained a large following as readers fell in love with my inspiring stories. The more I wrote, the more I gained strength to deal with the loss. Even though the articles were not paying much, they kept me busy and I did not have time to get lonely. By talking out my feelings to an audience I did not know, I had found a way to celebrate the gift that was my daughter. I had found a way to internalize my thoughts about her, and to draw comfort from the fact that no one was ever going to erase the memories of the unspeakable ways in which she touched my life.

The intense agony of loneliness that had previously overwhelmed and eaten me up became a thing of the past. Every day I became wiser and stronger. Even though I was alone, I became comfortable with it. Even though I could not replace my daughter, I found comfort in solitude when I learnt to externalize my pain. By doing things that brought me joy, I found great comfort in putting down my pain on a piece of paper. I do not know about other writers but I consider writing a gift of the Spirit, because in writing I connect so much with God and with other people. In writing I can have full pages of conversation with God. In writing, I find comfort and strength in times of pain and distress.

It was also in my loneliness that I learnt how to truly acknowledge God's presence. I would spend a lot of time in praise and worship. I began to see things from His perspective. It became a time to remind myself and to remind God of His promises, and I asked of him to honour them. I would break out in worship and sing new songs in His presence. I still have some of them, and even though I may never record them, I still use them in my personal devotion time. A time of great learning it was, I had finally realized that part of the reason I was feeling lonely is because of the God shaped void in my heart, and thankfully, God used that opportunity to draw me back to Himself and to revive my relationship with Him. In Psalms 42:5, we see the Psalmist asking himself "Why are you downcast, my soul?" and then immediately we see him encouraging himself to hope in his God, for he shall yet praise Him for the help of his countenance.

I learnt to be my own best friend, I learnt to love me, to be happy with me. I had spent considerable time hating myself, for not carrying my baby to term, for running away from God. I had destroyed myself by trying to over analyze everything that was happening to me, and trying to read too much into what people said, but in my loneliness, I had to just love me, I had no choice but to connect with me. Wayne Dyer once wrote that you cannot be lonely if you like the person you are alone with. In my loneliness I learnt to feel good about myself, I learnt to improve the person in me so that I could enjoy being with me. Self patience, self tolerance, and self love!

I have come to learn that everyone in the world goes through seasons of loneliness. The rich and the poor alike. The sick and the healthy alike. I believe I will not be wrong to say that some of the reasons the world is so chaotic is because of loneliness. People handle loneliness differently. Some opt to take drugs, some opt to take alcohol, while others opt to indulge in mindless sexual immorality starting off a path to self destruction.

Look around you and you will see crowds of people. They go about talking, talking and talking more, but rarely connecting with each other.

We live in a society where you cannot easily tell a lonely person by looking at their faces. Faces are just masks, hiding our deep feelings. There are many situations in life that can make us feel abandoned by God, by family and even friends. No matter what you are going through today, be encouraged that even though you feel like God isn't there, He is there.

In old times, the Lord was in the temple and He manifested His presence in many places. He manifested His presence to Moses in the burning bush. In Ezekiel 48: 35, after the land had been divided, the Lord spoke in a vision about the new name of the new city, the New Jerusalem that would be called 'Jehovah Shamma', meaning 'The Lord is There'. Not only was the Lord going to be in the temple, but His presence was going to fill the whole city.

When Shadrach, Meshach and Abednego were thrown into the fiery furnace, the Lord was there to rescue them. They did not get burnt. When Daniel was thrown into the lions den, the hungry lions did not devour him, because God was there with him. When Paul and Silas were thrown in a dungeon cell, the Lord was there with them. The Lord is there for you today even though you cannot see His face.

In Psalms 22, we see David in a moment of deep distress, crying out to God, asking God why he had forsaken him. In the Psalm that follows, Psalms 23, we see David, but this time proclaiming God's presence in his life, proclaiming that even though he walks through the valley of the shadow of death, he would fear no evil, because he surely knew that God was with him.

Matthew 27: 46 - 'Eloi, Eloi, lama sabachthani?' – meaning 'My God, my God, why have you forsaken me?'

Even Jesus Himself at some point felt abandoned by His Father. He felt abandoned when He was walking through the valley of the shadow of death. He therefore identifies with what you are going through today. If you are going through a valley of weeping, a valley of sorrow and untold pain, know that Jesus is there with you.

Jesus is our present companion in times of trouble. He is an ever present God. Before He ascended to heaven, He promised us that He will never leave us nor forsake us, that He will always be with us to the very end of age. He will always be there to reassure us, to comfort us, to guide us, to strengthen us, to make us prosper and to bless us.

When I lost my daughter I questioned where God was and why He didn't prevent it. I felt all alone, all abandoned and all forgotten despite the fact that I always had family and friends around me. It was like no one except me understood the bond that was between my baby and I. I was going through a blinding haze, not knowing where I was coming from or where I was going. It was hard for me to pray. Whenever I prayed for God to send me some quick relieve, whenever I attempted to touch God, I felt like all I was getting was dead silence.

But I now know better. Looking back I see how God was present every step of the way. Looking back I feel stupid for doubting God's faithfulness. I have now learnt that the feeling that God isn't there for us is just an illusion that our arch enemy the devil creates to make us question our God, so when you feel all abandoned, all alone, remember Jehovah Shamma! The Lord is there! Do not take His presence for granted because HIS PRESENCE IS HIS GREATEST PRESENT TO US NOW!!

You could be going through a season of loneliness as you read this. Maybe you have just lost your job and you are feeling so alone, maybe you have just relocated to another country or town where you do not know anyone and the loneliness is overwhelming. Maybe just like me you have just lost a loved one, a spouse maybe, a child. You could even be going through a divorce and you have now found yourself alone after years of being with someone. You do not have to sentence yourself to a jail, a solitary confinement. Whatever has happened in your life that has caused you to be lonely, do not allow it to take control over your life. Allow someone to reach out to you today. Some of us are lonely because of this mask that we put in front of others, we are not willing to let our friends know that we are lonely, we are not willing to connect with our friends. As a result, they cannot reach out to us since they cannot see the depth of our hearts. Choose today not to become a victim of your loneliness but instead choose to emerge a victor.

Remember the story of Hagar, the Egyptian slave who was Sarah's hand help. At Sarah's suggestion, she got pregnant by Abraham which caused so much tension in the household until she had to run away. She must have felt unwanted, unloved, alone in an alien land, and to make the situation worse, pregnant. In Genesis 16:13 we see her coming to the realization that she was not alone, that God was with her, so she called Him El Roi, the God who sees. This is the same God who wants you to know that you are indeed not alone, that He is with you, that He sees you. He may not be able to offer you a physical hug or a kiss, He may not be able to offer you a physical warm hand, but He is willing to offer you some words of encouragement, and if you listen carefully, you may just hear His still soothing comforting voice assuring you that you are precious in His sight, though it seems like no one cares. He does and He wants to remind you that He is Jehovah Shamma, and that in your loneliness, His presence is the greatest present to you!

SCRIPTURE FOCUS

2 Timothy 4:16-18

"At my first answer no man stood with me, but all men
forsook me: I pray God that it may not be laid to their
charge. Notwithstanding the Lord stood with me, and
strengthened me; that by me the preaching might be
fully known, and that all the Gentiles might hear: and
I was delivered out of the mouth of the lion. And the
Lord shall deliver me from every evil work, and will
preserve me unto His heavenly kingdom: to whom be
glory for ever and ever. Amen."

Chapter 4

A Season Of Letting Go And Letting God

MARY CARTER MIZRANY is the one who wrote in a song about a mother, that "... her heart becomes an altar, which holds each burden and care; and nothing moves the heart of God, more than a mother's prayer."

Ever since God gave me a daughter, ever since I learnt that I was pregnant, loving my baby became my life. Making sure that she would have everything that she needed became the reason why I would wake up every morning and go to work. She became the reason for my being, the reason for my breathing.

It therefore goes without saying that when I lost her letting go was the hardest thing for me. I held on to her as though she was still alive. Not a day passed without me wondering how different life would have been if she had been around. I totally refused to believe that I would let go of her and let God. That was out of the question. I knew I couldn't, I knew there was no way I was going to be able to do that.

The bible in Philippians 3:13 urges us to forget the past and look forward to what lies ahead of us. Two years now and counting, I have been able to do just that, let go of the past and embrace the future, let go and let God. With Jesus I have been able to let go, and let her be. And not just letting go of my daughter, but I have also been able to let go and let God in other aspects of my life too. Every day I am learning and striving to give over my own will to the will of God, am striving to give over my own desires and urges so as to sink down to that seed that God has sown in my heart, truly learning to deny myself and take up His easy yoke.

Just the other day I was thinking back the events of my life, and I started asking myself many questions. I had planned my life so much so that I thought that only death would stop me from achieving my goals. But it turned out that nothing in my plans was going to work as I had planned. Things started falling apart, and I found myself back to square one, with a lot of pain and heartache, wondering what rock I had built my life on that was falling apart so fast. For sure the storm had hit my 'house', the rains had descended, the winds had blown, the floods had come and burst against my house, my life and left me hanging on to life on a thread.

That is what led me to ask myself what God's will for my life was. Had I not involved God in my planning? Had I forgotten who God was? Had I stopped drawing my daily nourishment and sustenance from Him? Had I been doing things in my own strength instead of resting in Christ and listening to His plans for me? The events in my life brought me to a deeper understanding of Isaiah 14. This chapter talks about the falling down of Lucifer from heaven. In verse 13-15, it says, 'You said in your heart, "I will ascend to heaven; I will raise my throne above the stars of God; I will sit enthroned on the mount of assembly, on the utmost heights of the sacred mountain. I will ascend above the tops of the clouds; I will make myself like the Most High" But you are brought down to the grave, to the depths of the pit'.

If you study this scripture well, you will notice the ego and the pride in Lucifer trying to play God. Notice the many times he says 'I will....' Wanting to be more like God, even greater, and the result of this attitude was him being kicked out of heaven. Why? Because God does not tolerate any rival to His throne. Because He demands exclusive worship. He clearly demands in Exodus 20:3 that we shall have no other gods before Him. Much as today's culture puts a lot of weight and emphasis on self dependence, which is not a bad thing, but it becomes a bad thing when it is emphasized to a point of trying to be independent even from God. God is the same yesterday, today and forever. The same way He required us to trust in Him alone when we had very little is the same way He still requires us to trust in

Him even when we have much.

I kept meditating on these scriptures in Exodus, and even though I may not have intentionally set God aside in my planning, it was a very painful wake up call that made me re-examine my way of life in terms of God's involvement. I was going about life trying to mastermind every circumstance in my life, trying to control the uncontrollable, always trying to make my plans work. I had been so full of my own ideas, plans, schedules, and I was so determined to achieve my goals that I was not even willing to stop, look around and listen to His voice.

Deuteronomy 29:29 - "The secret things belong to the LORD our God, but those things which are revealed belong to us and to our children forever, that we may do all the words of this law.

So I wondered if what has been happening to me was His way of bringing me to a place of obedience in Him and a place of spiritual maturity. I wished I knew why God had let pain, suffering, disappointments and sadness take the centre of my life, but as sure as He lives, I knew He was also not obliged to explain Himself to me. I have also come to appreciate the importance of building my house upon a rock that is immovable, that rock who knows what tomorrow holds.

My frustrations were as a result of me trying to make things happen in the strength of my own flesh, me holding on to myself and my life when I was nothing but dust! For sometime I had developed this feeling that I knew better than He who speaks to the mountains, He who speaks to the oceans, He who spoke the whole universe into existence. The events in my life brought me to the humbling reminder that I have to let go and let God! I do not have to play God anymore. I was so focused on forcing my own will into my life that I had pushed aside the will of God in my life. I had even become afraid of praying God's will in my life because I was afraid that His will would contradict my will, and even when I prayed that His will be done, there never was that sincerity that it deserved. I knew that submitting to His will meant that my own will had to be overturned. It meant that God would have to be the one calling the shots always.

But God being God had to look for a way to make me yield to His control. He had to look for a way to restore my dependence on Him, to guard me against self-reliance. He had to make His will precede mine, and everything that I was going through were simply thorns of His planting. And after everything that happened, I came to a realization that I was unhappy simply because I was denying God's sovereignty and never surrendering to His control. I now know that all along God wanted the best for me. Even though I felt the frustrations of many unanswered prayers, I now know that God has a good plan for me, and this I do not doubt anymore. And although most times it seemed like I was put on this earth without a purpose, I know that with God in the lead, my future is safe and secure and I have a divine purpose to live for.

I am not alone. Since time immemorial, man has always struggled between leaning on his own flesh and strength, and leaning on the mighty power of God, never understanding that whatever God wants us to fulfil on this earth should be through His own strength. Let me take you back to the garden of Eden. Adam and Eve decided to eat the forbidden fruit. That was the first time in the history of man that man went against God's will. This is the time that man first ignored God's directives and decided to hold on to the notion that there was something better than God in this life.

A very funny thing is that even when I was going through all that, I would cry so much, like I wanted to manipulate God with my crying. Like I wanted my crying to move God so that He could answer my prayers faster. I would even rebel and try to force my way out of the problems. I tried listening to friends, most of whom by the way had no clue of the raging war inside me since they could not discern that this one was a war between God and I. But God being God would immediately cut off any means of help except through Him. He wanted me to rely solely on Him.

Are you in the same position that I was in? Struggling with God's will for your life like I was? Guess what? You do not have to know what the future holds for you, because God will take you one step at a time, He will reveal His will for your life one step at a time. The bible says that His Word is a lamp to your feet and a light for your path. This light may not illuminate your whole future, but it sure does shed some light as to your next step. Do not be afraid of praying that God's will be done in your life, quit being afraid that what His answer might not be what you want, let Him be God!

All that God is asking us to do is to simply surrender our lives to Him, our thoughts, our plans, our personal desires, and yield to His will. In doing so, He shall supply us with sufficient grace, and strength to keep up as His plan for our lives unfold. I am not saying that you do not have a say in your life; no, in fact, our Lord is gracious enough to give us a free will, and it pleases Him to see us make personal choices between several possibilities, but His desire is that we make our choices in accordance to His will, and because He is the one who fulfils the desires of our hearts, He shall surely supply us with the peace of mind even when we do not understand what His next step is, for He surely will not reveal the whole plan to us, but will instead reveal it to us one step at a time. It is when we start bucking against His will and forcing our own plans that we find ourselves frustrated and running out of strength. So choose today to let go of your will and fully submit to His.

I don't know what it is that you are holding so tightly in your hands that there is no room for God's will in your life, something that you want so badly and may not want to really know if God really wants you to have it. Are you holding on so tightly to that girl or boyfriend of yours that you don't want to know if He or she is the one that God wants you to have? Are you holding on to your job so tightly because you think it is the key to your prosperity that you have forgotten that God is the giver of it all? Are you so prosperous that you have forgotten who brought you thus far? You have to let go of all that is separating you from God's will and let God. You have to let go of that hatred and unforgiveness that has chained your heart and held you from God's happiness.

Most of us hold on so tightly to the things that we love and value, our families, our careers, our health, our education, our possessions, and even to life itself. It is time that we realize that the very things that we so tightly hold on to belong to our God, and if you want to exalt those things above God, He sure has a way of claiming them back from us. He is ready to orchestrate the affairs of your life so as to bring His will back to your life, such that there will be nothing else left except Him alone!! He will empty your hands completely and fill them with Himself. Everything that we own is loaned to us and He has the right to take them away as at when He feels is right and beneficial to all. Today when I approach His throne, I completely let go of my credentials and my ability to pull strings here and there, I approach Him with nothing in my hands, and simply cling to His cross for grace.

As I look back, I now proclaim that I was crushed between the millstones like an olive, that I may yield nothing but the oil of submissiveness. I now glory in my tribulations knowing fully well that though I was bruised, I have yielded to God a precious grain in His garden, and can now come humbly to His presence with the strength of His grace and tell Him to have His way in my life, oh that His will be done in my life! I have now learnt that all these were light afflictions, fashioned to be my stepping stones leading me to the path of a higher ground in my obedience to God, a higher ground of higher and greater faith, a higher ground of higher and greater trust, higher and greater love, and higher and greater dependence on my God. It has been from His healing touch that I have become closer to Him than ever. It is through all these multi-coloured stepping stones that others are now able to look at me and see a big God, a faithful God, a God who does what He says He will do!

My grip on my earthly plans was so tight that it had to take some disappointments for me to take a breather and question who the driver of my life was, and who was shepherding me. I had become my own shepherd and God in His own infinite wisdom had to break me to remind me that He is the true shepherd, the shepherd that gave His life to save me, all this just so that He could draw me closer to His bosom; all this so that He could give me a second chance to walk with Him. It was only in my brokenness, in my suffering, in my crying that I could finally see His outstretched hands to me offering me physical, emotional and spiritual healing, forgiveness, love and mercy.

Judges 18:24 - "You have taken away my gods which I made.",

Our faith has taught us that one of the greatest sins that man can commit is trying to be in charge, in control of our own lives without involving God, and a wise man once said that happy are those people who hold on lightly to the things that they value greatly. So if you do not want to cry like Micah, learn to hold all things loosely as though you do not have them. Do not be afraid to let go, God has the greater picture and already knows where you will be 20 years from today (even though He may not tell it. His will for your life is perfect. Realize that you were created with a divine purpose, and you have to let God be on the throne for you to live a happy, and fulfilled life. All you have to do is yield to His control, yield to His leading, Let Go And Let God!!!

For many people, "Let go and let God" is just but a catchy phrase that is on everyone lips ready for use whenever someone is having some kind of trouble. For me, letting go and letting God is a powerful phrase, whose depth in meaning and in day to day application to life's struggles is totally important. The phrase has now taken an entirely new meaning to me, and whenever I hear someone say let go and let God, the first thing that comes to mind is "Get out of God's way, and let Him be God". Looking back today, I cannot stop asking God, "who am I that you are so mindful of me?" because everything I have gone through has worked out for my good. I have learnt to say just like Job that though He slay me, yet will I trust in Him.

If you are reading my story and you see a reflection of yourself, well, I have a word just for you. Just the same way I have learnt to obey God through the bitter experiences that I have gone through recently, you too can learn to let these sufferings and light afflictions bring you closer to God simply by letting go, and letting Him be God! God can only live through you only if you let Him, if you learn to get your strength from Him, if you learn to ask Him to reveal to you the plans that He has for your life, if you learn to rest in Him alone, if you learn to trust in Him when every one else has put their trust in their horses and their chariots.

It is high time you and I learnt to tell Him every morning that Lord, this is your day, let your will be done in our lives!! Oh how He longs to give you joy everlasting if only you let Him. How He longs to give you the sun, moon and the stars of the skies. Oh how He longs to pull you out of that darkness that you are in right now, if only you can break before Him and ask Him to take control. If only you knew that His plans for you are to give you the ecstasies of heaven, to shower you with His favour.

My dear brother, my dear sister, these worldly pressures are way too much for your feeble shoulders. You cannot make it on your own. You cannot let God take a back seat in your life anymore. There are so many things that can and do go wrong in this world. The cares, the stress, the pressures, the disappointments, the tests, broken hearts, broken dreams, and you are just a man! You've got to let go and let God! You have got to totally surrender. If only you can let Him take charge so that you can live in this world but still have one foot in the heavenly realm, and then you would experience the joys of trusting your plans to the master planner of the universe. Then you would know the bounties that He has in store for you, bounties beyond your wildest fantasies.

We must learn not to be too secluded in our plans to have a good life, we must quit looking inwardly to ourselves, but must instead learn to look up to our God and walk down the path of His perfect will, for He shall make you go from strength to strength and make you feel His favour and blessings upon your life. He says that those very things that you are holding on to, if you let go of them now, you will soon look back and realize that they are the weights that the Lord has turned into wings that will help you soar high up to heights that you never dreamed possible, things that no eye has seen, no ear has heard! He is asking you this day to put your trust in Him, trust Him with your life, trust Him with your career, trust Him with your family, trust Him with your business, He is asking you to trust Him in your heartache and despair. Oh! He says, if only you would be willing to say right now," not my will, but yours be done!"

What is it that you are holding on to? What is it that is binding you? Is it pain, hurt, rejection, betrayal, disappointments? God is telling you to let go, just let go. Why do you want to let anything destroy the good plans that the Lord has in store for you? Why are you letting people or things control your destiny?

A story is told of a man who was taking a walk on a beautiful evening but he became so absorbed in his own thoughts that he wondered off and eventually found himself lost. Night was fast approaching, and it was also getting very cold. Time passed by and within no time it was very dark. He hastened his steps and then suddenly he tumbled and fell down but he managed to get hold of a branch. He was now hanging on a branch with no way of climbing back up. When he looked down all he saw was total darkness. He cried out for help but no one came to his aid. He then cried to God and promised God that if He saved him, He would always believe in Him. Then he heard a voice telling him " Just trust me, and let go of the branch, I've got you!" This must have sounded silly to the man, but that is exactly what God is asking you to do as you read this. He is asking you to trust Him no matter how silly and stupid His word might sound to you. He is asking you to let go and let Him.

Well, out of desperation, the man decided to let go since he really had no choice. Moments later he found himself on solid ground, not hurt since the ground which he fell on was actually not as deep as he had feared. But what was more beautiful was that he fell right back onto the path which was his route back home. There is always a fear in letting go and abandoning the control you have over your life, but there is also an overwhelming and liberating truth in acknowledging that you are not in control, that God is. Are you willing to trust God like this man, release your grip and approach His throne today having let go of everything in your hands, holding on to entirely nothing, and just tell Him "Nothing in my hands I bring, I simply cling to thee for grace".

SCRIPTURE FOCUS

Psalms 127 1-2

Unless the LORD builds the house, its builders labour in vain. Unless the LORD watches over the city, the watchman stand guard in vain. In vain you rise early and stay up late, toiling for food to eat, for He grants sleep to those He loves.

Proverbs 16:9

"A man's heart plans his way, but the LORD directs his steps."

Jeremiah 29:11

"For I know the thoughts that I think toward you, says the LORD, thoughts of peace and not of evil, to give you a future and a hope."

Chapter 5

A Season Of Being Still & Knowing That He Is God

*A*FTER THE ACCIDENT I went on a wild goose chase trying to over-analyze everything to see what may have compromised my baby's life. Even after the doctor had clearly explained what could have happened I still found myself coming up with reasons of my own. I thought about my eating habits, I thought about my movements, that I was overworking myself. I troubled myself so much with these thoughts as though they were going to bring my daughter back. At the end of the day all that I got from my goose chase was more trouble; hopelessness, stress, emotional breakdown and more chaos. Not at any one time did I even think of just being still.

They say that among the leading causes of killer diseases is anxiety. Everyone is anxious about something. Some are anxious about their marriages, others are anxious about their careers, others are anxious about their businesses. Naturally, we worry about what tomorrow holds for us, we are anxious about our futures. We very much want to have a peek of our tomorrow today that we end up throwing our systems out of order. This is because man was not created to worry or to be anxious, but in His wisdom God created man to trust Him all the time and not to be anxious about anything.

We find it hard to relax, we find it hard to wait for an outcome. The pressures of life are too much especially in a fast moving world. We panic easily, we chicken out and end up breaking under pressures. We have become professional worriers instead of warriors. Things are usually bad enough even without us worrying about them so worrying only makes the situation worse. By worrying you allow something to revolve around your mind over and over again without coming up with any meaningful solution to your problem. By worrying you let the enemy steal your joy and peace. You toss and turn in bed, lacking sleep and causing health dangers to your body worrying yourself sick.

The main reason we worry is because we are not patient enough with God to solve our problems. We want Him to solve our problems today and now. We want Him to bless us today and now. We want Him to heal us today and now. We want Him to open doors for us today and now. We more often than not forget that a life worth living is never rushed, and that we should give life a chance to unfold the way it is meant to unfold.

Some of us when we are confronted by a challenge, we cannot even be still for a day. We usually will call our best friend and talk it out with them, but sometimes all that God wants is for us to be still in Him, for us to rest in His care, for us to let Him give us the victory. Most times what He wants is for us to let Him speak to us and to give us peace and not to go running to our friends, but we are so impatient that we are unable to stay still and wait for His voice. It is not always that God will provide you with a friend whose shoulder you can cry on, because it is Him that He wants you to lean on, it is Him that He wants you to focus on, so be still, and know that He is God.

How many of us are guilty of trying to solve all life's problems? We are guilty of trying to control the outcome of every situation and can never sit back and let things follow their own course? How many of us are so guilty of trying to play 'judge, jury and executioner'? Sometimes we want something so bad that waiting is not an option. We get so restless and eager to 'get on with it'. We are more often than not unable to persevere in the face of delay. We get easily annoyed and upset when provoked. Some of us want immediate gratification so much that we get busy trying to help God run the universe!!

In other words, most of us lack patience. Yet the bible tells us that patience is a fruit of the Holy Spirit. What??? Does the bible mean to tell me that I should stay in the queue for as long as the circumstance dictates? That I should stay mum when every bone in my being wants to lash back in anger and in frustration? That I should sacrifice my feelings and my thoughts even when I know that I am on the right and the other party is on the wrong? Why not? If Job did it, why cant we? Job was tested beyond what most of us have gone through. He lost everything he owned and his loved ones, but he was able to stay patient, and even when his wife advised him to curse God, he did not.

Isaiah 30: 15 - For thus says the Lord God, the Holy One of Israel: "In returning and rest you shall be saved; in quietness and confidence shall be your strength..."

Isaiah 40: 31 - "But those who wait on the Lord shall renew their strength; they shall mount up with wings like eagles; they shall run and not be weary, they shall walk and not faint."

Many are the times that we have tried so hard to look for answers, and then God just tells us to "Be still and know that I am God..." This means that we totally surrender the situation into God's hands, that we lay all our burdens at His feet. And knowing that He is God means that we solely focus on His sovereignty, on His power, and His grace. To be still and know that He is God means that we give Him full control. It is naturally very hard to wait, because our natural instincts are always instructing us 'to do', 'to run', 'to react'. It takes a lot of patience to stay still, to stop talking, to stop planning, to stop running. It takes patience to just wait and listen, without being tense or frustrated.

There are times that I feel I need patience more than anyone else. I am the type that tries to figure out everything, trying to understand everything. My mind is so analytical that sometimes I end up filling in the gaps with answers that cause me pain, answers that cost me friends. I look too much for answers in the natural realm. Being still is a really big command for me. Just shutting off my mind and shutting up my fears so as to listen to

God as He speaks is a big challenge for me. But I am glad that I am a work in progress, a day at a time, step by step, and soon I will be a very patient person, willing to be still and to let God be God in all my circumstances.

James 1:4 - "But let patience have its perfect work, that you may be perfect and complete, lacking nothing."

So what exactly is patience? Longsuffering I would say, endurance, tolerance, forbearance under difficult circumstances. The bible has time and time again required us to be patient, to wait upon God, to be still. This shows us that patience should therefore be a way of thinking about, and responding to difficult situations. The patient response is rooted in our faith, because we are confident that the difficult situation will only last awhile. This patience is not just a feeling, but a decision and a will to endure. It is an attitude. We however need the wisdom of God so as not to let patience turn us into cowards. If anything, patience should make us more confident.

The bible requires us to not be anxious about anything, but in everything, by prayer and petition, with thanksgiving, present our requests to God. And the peace of God which transcends all understanding will guard our hearts and our minds in Christ Jesus. Without the peace of God, you will loose your patience and more often than not find yourself lashing out in anger at the people around you, and / or even at God Himself.

If you find yourself struggling with patience, do not lose hope. Patience is not instantaneously bestowed on us. Maybe you are struggling to put up with others, you may be working hard not to lose your temper, or maybe you are even struggling to trust in God. Well, I have good news for you! Patience is a quality that grows in the midst of our difficult circumstances. It is through these struggles that God teaches us patience. So you are some 'work-in-progress', God is not done with you yet!! But on your part, you can in the meantime learn to discipline your thoughts, pray for the ability to cope with different situations, and you will soon realize that your patience will achieve more than your force. There is a Dutch saying that says that a handful of patience is worth more than a bushel of brains. Proverbs 14:29 says that "The patient man shows much good sense, but the quick tempered man displays folly at its height."

The Lord wants us to wait on Him in prayer in whatever situation that we are in, so that He can fill us with His strength. This means that we should submit our thoughts, as well as our wills to Him, and let His will overtake ours, instead of taking matters into our own hands. A certain Chinese proverb says that one moment of patience may ward off great disaster, and one moment of impatience may ruin a whole life. Case in point, many of us are guilty of throwing away jobs that could have taken us to great heights had we waited a little bit longer.

We have thrown away careers that fit us so perfectly simply because we were not patient with ourselves, our colleagues or even our bosses. We have encountered difficult people in our work places, people who are hard to get along, but instead of being patient what have we done? We usually end up complaining, we become sour, we harbour grudges, we try to change everything that is happening around us, but rarely do we ask God to make us more patient and more tolerant of others. When things at work don't change as we want them to, some of us have ended up resigning, losing a chance for God to work in us, because most times, we are the ones who need to change and not our colleagues. God cannot work in us when we keep running away from situations; He can only work in us when we are still. We can only bloom where we are planted.

We have sacrificed relationships that were meant to be, simply because the other party was not changing as fast or as thoroughly as we want them to change or even because they do not have the strengths that we have or would like them to have. We wanted to see them change so fast that we forgot that we can only see change if we sit still and give them a chance to be themselves. We more often than not loose our patience with people who don't do things the way we want them done, we make people fit into our moods, and we try to make people be like us instead of giving them room to be what God created them to be. Instead of being still and appreciating them for what they are, we get busy trying to fix them. Our job is not to fix them, but to be patient with them, to be still and to know that He is God.

Psalms 46:10 - Be still, and know that I am God; I will be exalted among the nations, I will be exalted in the earth!

There is always a season for everything, a season for sowing and a season for reaping, a season for moving and a season for waiting. It is during this season of waiting that God wants us to be still. In a relationship, there has to be that time where you have to be still and wait for the relationship to get better, not run away. In your job, there has to be that time of waiting for a promotion, as opposed to resigning. So why can't we be still and know that He is God? Why cant we be still and let God be God?

Over time I have come to learn that in easy times patience is easy, and in difficult times, patience is difficult, almost impossible. Growing up as a girl from a poor family I had to be patient with my parents whenever I needed something that always seemed impossible for my parents to provide. I had to be patient with children from well off families. This was never easy. Now a grown up, I often must be patient with my boss, my colleagues, customers, my land lord, and pretty much every one that I come across. I am learning to be patient because the bible tells me that good things come to those who wait.

I am also learning to be patient with myself, just the same way that God is long suffering and patient with me. If God had not been patient with me, I would be long gone, I would past tense,

I would be lost. Time after time I find myself getting annoyed at myself over things that I have done wrongly, wrong decisions that have affected my life, and I sometimes find it hard to even forgive myself. This, self-patience, has so far been the hardest form of patience for me to develop.

When I was in mourning, I would try to relive the days before the accident, and always thought that if I had things differently, if I would not have had the accident, and my baby would not have died. I even thought that I would not have been a good mother and maybe that is why God took my baby from me, and I kept doing this self condemnation thing for quite a while. No matter how much I kept shouting to myself to get over the feeling, I found it too hard to develop that self-patience.

All my emotional strength was gone and I had no strength for patience. I punished myself by putting myself through a really tough time of self blame. My mind strayed a lot and I felt like I did not have the capacity to choose what to think about. The thoughts of my inability to carry my daughter to term consumed me. I was totally lost in despairing thoughts. Being impatient with myself drained my inner strength. This lack of self-patience brought along with it the lack of self-acceptance. It seemed like my own self value had totally diminished. I felt like I was not important to anyone. It took spending time with God alone for me to develop that self-patience. It was after this that I finally felt that I was important to my family, I was important to God and that is why He had saved my life. I fully well know that there can never be another substitute for me in the lives of those that I love.

Spending time with God allowed me to tell Him of all my fears and concerns. It helped me let Him bear all my sorrows and pains, it helped me lay all my disappointments at His feet, and finally accept His healing. It opened my eyes to the revelation that I am only a work in progress, that God is not done with me yet. I am now more patient with myself, and I am more patient with the people in my life, and those that I come across in this journey.

So I now know why patience is a fruit of the Holy Spirit... because nothing less than the Spirit of God Himself can cause me to maintain my calm when I clearly know I should be on the rampage!! Only the Spirit of God can cause me to be still and know that He is God. I have so far quit trying to understand God and why He tells me to be still. I have so far learnt that He actually doesn't want me to understand Him, all He wants from me is obedience.

SCRIPTURE FOCUS

Psalms 46:1-11

God is our refuge and strength, an ever-present help in trouble,

Therefore we shall not fear, though the earth give way, and the mountains fall into the heart of the sea,

Though its waters roar and foam and the mountains quake with their surging.

There is a river whose streams make glad the city of God, the holy place where the Most High dwells.

God is within her, she will not fall; God will help her at break of day.

Nations are in uproar, kingdoms fall; He lifts His voice, the earth melts.

The Lord Almighty is with us; the God of Jacob is our fortress.

Come and see the works of the Lord, the desolations He has brought on the earth,

He makes wars cease to the ends of the earth; He breaks the bow and shatters the spears, He burns the shield with fire.

"Be still and know that I am God; I will be exalted among the nations, I will be exalted in the earth."

The Lord Almighty is with us; the God of Jacob is our fortress.

Chapter 6

My Extremity – My Wilderness – Became God's Opportunity

*M*OST OF US have gone through the most heart-rending seasons of extremity, seasons of wilderness in our lives, maybe in our careers, our marriages, our families, our businesses etc. These seasons make us question if the God who parted the red seas for the Israelites and promised them a land of abundance is still the same God we serve today, we wonder if there really is a way out of our wilderness. We have lost loved ones, some of our loved ones are lying hopelessly on hospital beds waiting for a miracle. Maybe we are wondering whether to believe the doctor's report or God's report. Some of us have lost possessions that we held so dear to us. We may have lost our jobs just when we needed them most. We may be feeling like our world is falling apart. We feel like God has abandoned us and life has lost meaning. We have so many questions.

About 4 months before I lost my baby, I had lost someone very close to me, a man who by all means I consider my father, a man who I would not like to talk much about here, but bottom line is he was my hero, he was the man that I looked up to in life. He was physically crippled but he had beaten all odds to become a very successful man. He died suddenly at his prime. A few months before he died, he had given me a 2-bedroomed house and one of his pick-ups for business. Unfortunately by the time he died he had not registered the property in my name so I was not able to claim them after his death.

I didn't know that this was just another of the several losses that I was going to encounter. I then had a very good job and when I was still recovering, I was approached by a friend who needed some cash badly, he lied to me that his father was sick, he was able to convince me to give him some cash which he was to pay me. At the end of the day he did not pay me, I went into depression because it was a lot of money. Things spiralled out of control, one thing led to another and I ended up losing my job. With my savings running low, I became more and more desperate. I was able to find a job shortly afterwards but unfortunately my body was not strong enough especially because I was to be stationed in a very remote and rocky area. I ended up resigning after the first day out of the pains from my Caesarian Section wound, which had been aroused by the rocky morning and evening drive.

I had previously bought myself a plot in Kitengela expecting to build my mum a house, but I had to give up the plot so as to pay up a debt. I found myself completely wanting and desperate. I got a part time job writing for a local newspaper and while I put so much effort into it hoping it would help pay my bills, I was so disappointed when the newspaper started delaying my payments, and what was worse was probably the fact that even the rates would be re-adjusted to the lower side, even after my articles were published. I therefore became frustrated and stopped writing actively.

All this time the bills were running high, and friends were distancing themselves from me, only a handful remained. I truly thank God for those few friends and family members who stuck with me through it all. Some went as far as paying my rent without asking that I pay them back when I get a job. Others would stock my fridge with foodstuffs. In all my ten years of working, I had never found myself so desperate. I was used to being so independent that before then I did not know how it felt like to have someone do my shopping. I had heard of boyfriends who shop for their girlfriends, but for me that was just that, stories.

I had never been shopped for, or as those who know me would say, I had never allowed any man to shop for me. So you can now imagine how hard it was for me to find myself in a situation where I had to almost beg. But my extremity became God's opportunity to prove His faithfulness to me. There would be times when I would be broke to my last coin, and miraculously someone would pay me a visit and re-stock my fridge. God was so faithful to me because I do not remember any day that I lacked food, or a day when I was unable to pay rent.

This was the most trying moment of my adult life. In summary, in a span of six months only, I lost a man I call dad, I lost my daughter, I lost my job, I lost my plot, a house, a pick-up van, my savings, and I also lost my friends (well, now I know they never were real friends). Just how extreme could it get? How drier could my wilderness get? I had a million and one questions. Why did it have to be me, when there are so many evil doers out there who are having a good trial-free life? How was I to trust God to enlarge my territories when I was losing everything, one after the other?

Genesis 22:14 - "And Abraham called the name of the place, The-Lord-Will-Provide (Jireh); as it is said to this day, "In the Mount of The Lord it shall be provided." (Parentheses added)

I have been meditating on the word of God and the other day I thought about Abraham. Abraham was a servant of God, a friend of God, but that did not exempt him from facing trials. He was tested beyond what most of us have endured. Despite the many promises that God had made about making him a great nation and increasing him, God asked him to sacrifice his one and only son.

Abraham must have asked himself so many questions. How was he ever to become a great nation with his only son dead? What explanation would he give to Sarah for killing the son she had been blessed with in her old age? What would the community think of a leader who had killed his own son? All these questions and more must have crossed Abraham's mind.

A lot of possible answers must also have crossed his mind. Maybe God would raise his son from the dead. Maybe God would vindicate him by justifying his obedience to Him. But he made up his mind that he was going to obey God no matter what. So he went ahead and prepared the altar as per God's instructions. When his son asked him where the sacrificial lamb was, he answered that the Lord Himself would provide.

And just at his deepest hour of need, when he took the knife to slay his son, the Lord called him and told him not to kill his son, and a ram came out of a thicket and he sacrificed the ram as a burnt offering to God. Genesis 22:14 says "...And Abraham called the name of that place 'Jehovah Jireh', or 'The Lord will provide'. And to this day it is said, "on the mountain of the Lord, the Lord shall provide". Saying that the Lord will provide means that the Lord will see to it.

Philipians 4:19 - "And my God shall supply all your need according to His riches in glory by Christ Jesus."

You maybe lacking right now, but I assure you that on the mountain of the Lord, the Lord Himself shall provide, and will see to it that you shall not be ashamed. You may be hard pressed on every side, but the Lord shall see to it that you are not crushed. You may be persecuted, but the Lord will see to it that you are not abandoned. He will not disown His word.

Maybe you are jobless and your finances are running out, the Lord God will see to it that you shall not go hungry. You may have lost your properties, your prized possessions, but the Lord will see to it that your loss is re-compensated. If your difficulties multiply and there seems to be no way out, the Lord will see to it that the mountains are levelled before you and the way shall be cleared for you.

Just like Abraham, your provision will come in the time of your extremity because man's extremity is God's opportunity, and God's full manifestation may be delayed till your darkest hour has come. Don't you know that it is darkest just before dawn? Abraham knew that pretty well. Remember a time that you have been tested in the past, but God saw you through. God is not less than He was then. He is the same yesterday, today and forever more. If He provided for you then, He will provide for you now.

At that time when your need is pressing urgently, when it seems that it is at its worst, then the Lord will provide a ram. In His own time, God will deliver you. Your work is to ask by prayer and to act by faith, and you will see God in your want. Approach the mountain of God knowing that the Lord shall provide.

Struggling with school fees? The Lord will see to it. Struggling with house rent? The Lord will see to it. Struggling with hospital bills? The Lord will see to it. Struggling to put a meal on the table? The Lord will see to it. This is because He is the Lord who provides, the one who sees and knows your need.

Even at a time when our nation and the whole world at large is going through a financial crisis, choose to believe that even if a thousand fall at your side, and ten thousand at your right hand, that they will not come near you. Believe that God will not fail in His word. The same God who promised Isaac that He would provide for him, that He would make him flourish even in times of famine is the same God today, for He is the same yesterday, today and forever.

After all is said and done, you will find cause to call the name of every place of trial, Jehovah Jireh and raise an everlasting memorial of Gods providence. These places of trials will always remind you that the trials of our life prove the strength of our anchor!

SCRIPTURE FOCUS

Psalm 37:25

I have been young, and now am old; yet have I not seen
the righteous forsaken, nor his seed begging bread.

Luke 12:7

But even the very hairs of your head are all numbered.
Fear not therefore: ye are of more value than many
sparrows.

2Corinthians 9:8

And God is able to make all grace abound toward you;
that ye, always having all sufficiency in all things, may
abound to every good work:

Philippians 4:19

But my God shall supply all your need according to His
riches in glory by Christ Jesus.

Chapter 7

A Thorn Of His Planting?

WHY? WHY? WHY? So many 'whys' and not many 'becauses'. Do you sometimes ask yourself this question? Not understanding why things are happening the way they are happening? Wondering if the God of Abraham and the God of Isaac and Jacob, is still your God? Wondering if the God who made a way for the Israelites across the Red Sea, the God who saved Meshach, Shadrach and Abednego from the fiery furnace is still the God of today? I have been there, done that, and came out with a revelation.

Do you sometimes wonder if you are still serving the same God who in the older days would answer prayers with pearls of thunder and bolts of lightning? You call on Him day and night, but He seems to be deaf? Just the other day a friend called me up, asking me to take it upon myself to pray for her because she had wept and prayed and earnestly sought God's will, but she was convinced that God was not hearing her prayers anymore. Yes, we all go through such phases in our lives. The more we pray, the more silent God becomes, a thundering silence that brings nothing but agony to you.

Over the years I have come to realize that with God, nothing happens by chance, that nothing happens to us, but that it happens for us. And even though most of the times when something bad happens to us, we usually tend to think that it has also caught God by surprise, I now know that nothing happens to me without His knowledge. I now know that there is a larger purpose for the bad things that happen to us, and the only time we will be able to know and understand that purpose is when you are ready and open minded enough to receive it. His word tells me that He has engraved my name on the palm of His hand, that He may not forget me, and this knowledge gives me the strength to soldier on, knowing that He is in it after all. He constantly reminds me that He is a God of love and great mercy, whose mercies towards me extend to the heavens.

James 1:2 - "My brethren, count it all joy when you fall into various trials..."

There have been extremely painful moments in my life, moments of hellfire, damnation, problems, sorrow and pain, moments that I have felt like God has left me just at the very moment that I needed Him most. At times strong storms of life have blown me around, tossed me from side to side, and carried me to and fro with these winds of distress and adversity. But I knew it was at those times that God would call me to rejoice in my pain, to consider it pure joy, knowing that the testing of my faith was going to produce perseverance, and perseverance was going to build my character, and character, hope.

It has been in these tough times that I have come to fully know and understand His comforting embrace, the warmth of His arms, as He would gently ask of me to rest my head upon His shoulders. It was in these times that I have learnt the solace of His love, and the peace that flows from His heart to mine, filling me and taking my spirit to the heavenly realms from where I see all these problems from a new light, just as He sees them. He has taught me to let Him comfort me and to accept His peace, even as He lets me know that even though the periods that I am in pain may seem like a long time, it is only a moment compared to eternity.

I have come to appreciate that my trials are responsible for my growth, that the more I am pressed, the more I am empowered, that adversity has actually been to my advantage. I may not look like much today, but it is because God is not yet done with me, I am a work in progress! Maybe you or even I, may not like what I see in me today, but I still have great hope for the future, and for this I choose to appreciate every trial that comes my way. I know that the Lord will chip deep into me so as to conform me into His image. I still realize that I have along way to go, but that is the least of my concerns, what matters is that I realize the purpose for my trials. After every trial, I will rise up, dust myself off, and learn what God wants me to learn and bounce back.

I have learnt to trust God to prune me, and prune me accordingly, to propel me towards my God chosen purpose in life. If there is anything in me that might prevent me from achieving that which God has in store for me, I readily ask the Lord to prune me. It definitely is not an easy road to take, but I know that before I was formed in my mother's womb, the Lord knew my future, and He set me apart, and if pruning is the way to keep me in that course, then be it. If this kind of pruning is necessary on me, then I know that it is an instruction sent in pure heavenly love, only because He cares for His own.

Job 23:10 - "But He knows the way I take; when He has tested me, I shall come forth as gold".

When Job was going through the toughest and biggest trial of his life, he asked God for the reason why he had to go through all that, and God responded by asking Job, "Where were you when I laid the foundations of the earth? Tell me, if you understand. Who marked off its dimensions? On what were its footings set, or who laid its cornerstone while the morning star sang together and all the angels shouted for joy? After all this, Job was confident.

Despite going through the toughest time of his life, despite being tried and tested beyond any kind of reasoning, besides all the sicknesses, and despite losing his home, his wealth, his wife, his children, his livestock, and all that was of value to him, God still favoured Job. But not only was he just favoured, but he was favoured with so much more!! The bible says that when Job recognized and acknowledged God as being sovereign and greater than what he had lost, God favoured him so much that the bible says, that Job's latter glory was greater than his former!

What more shall we say? Our Lord God knows what you are going through. He is not sleeping on the job. Whatever is happening to you is not a mistake, it has a divine purpose. Don't you know that you belong to God and His name is tattooed on your very soul and engraved deep on your heart? He is touched by the feeling of your infirmities. His heart breaks to see you in pain and in struggle. He hurts when you are feeling forsaken, hopeless, lost and abandoned. So stay strong in the Lord, keep your faith, and the Lord will use these difficulties to grow you, stretch you and propel you to higher levels.

Do you remember that it was when Joseph was sold by his brothers as a slave that his talent in interpreting dreams was discovered? Elisabeth Kubler once said that the most beautiful people are those who have known defeat, known suffering, known struggle, known loss, and have found their way out of the depths. These persons have an appreciation, a sensitivity and an understanding of life that fills them with compassion, and a deep concern. She said that beautiful people do not just happen! We therefore have to stop protecting ourselves 'from God' so to speak, let us quit running away from that which the Lord deems necessary. We have to come to a point where we totally give in to what the Lord wants to make us, a time when we have to break before Him and sing *"I surrender all, I surrender all, all to thee my blessed Saviour, I surrender all!"*

The bible tells us that the Lord will not allow us to be tempted beyond what we can endure, in 1st Corinthians 10:13, that no temptation has seized us except that which is common to man. Our duty is to lean on the Lord, and as we do that we shall discover that His faithfulness shall remain even as He teaches us to discover more about His purpose in our trials. The Lord Himself understands the pain and the depth of feelings of loss, even feelings of being betrayed, remember He Himself was abandoned by those He loved most, and betrayed by His own, with a kiss. Remember how He even prayed to the Father that the cup of suffering may be removed from Him. He understands your physical pain. On the cross, He cried in agony as the nails pierced His hands and feet, even to a point of thinking that His Father had forsaken Him.

Some of us have in the past believed that we go through trials and temptations because we have wronged God; we have come to equate trials to sin. It is not so, and I take courage in knowing that even our Lord Jesus, who was without sin, was tempted and tried. The devil is the architect of the lie that trials should be equated to sin, and He wants you to believe that the trials and temptations are your punishment. Don't you give in to this lie, the Lord is on your side, He will give you whatever it is that you need to come out as a victor. When it comes to pruning, even the good branch is pruned so as to make it bear more fruit. Maybe you consider yourself a prayer warrior, still, when the Lord wants to take you to a higher level in your praying, He might prune you so as to raise you to the level that He desires of you.

2Corinthians 12:9 - "And He said to me, "My grace is sufficient for you, for My strength is made perfect in weakness."

Paul had been having what we would call thorns in the flesh, and he prayed that these may depart from Him, but we see that God had other plans for him. These thorns were not removed from him, but instead, God promised him sufficient grace to endure all, because God's power is made perfect in weakness. It is when Paul understands this that he finally accepts God's plan with joy, the thorns of His planting! Sometimes we do not need to tear ourselves away from the thorn, or even to tear the thorn out of our flesh, maybe God wants us to simply pray that He gives us patience and strength to endure the thorn, and to remind us that His grace is sufficient for us in all manner of trial.

I do not know what your fears are but it could be that it is through those fears that the Lord may choose to reveal Himself to you. This was so in the case of the disciples. We read in the bible how Jesus asked them to go over to the other side of the lake, and while in the boat, a fierce storm was raging. The disciples feared and were afraid for their lives, but it is here when all hope was gone that Jesus revealed His power over the storm. He wants you to fix your eyes on Him and trust Him whenever you are tempted to fear and worry. He wants you to keep trusting Him whenever you feel so overwhelmed that the tears just flow freely. Our Lord wants you to trust in His ability to lead you and guide you even in the darkest night. It is much easier to put your hand into His hand and let Him lead than it is to try and find your own path and possibly stumble along the way.

If you are going through a trial whose purpose you still do not know yet, the answer lies in searching and seeking the Lord, and as you seek and find Him, He shall reveal it to you. Maybe the miracle in your trial is like a tiny mustard seed that is hidden deep within your heart. It may not be visible to you now, but one day you will come to realize the reason for your trial, for it will be put in the open, a spectacular display of the miracle in your trial. Every trial will uncover a layer of self that you did not know, and help you identify a depth of soul that you did not know. What you can be sure of is that if Christ has put you in that trial, if that thorn is one of His own planting, then He has weighed you, He knows what it will cost you, He knows how much grace you need, but most importantly, He knows the reward He has in store for you.

Do you know that in the book of Exodus 16:4, the Lord told Moses that He would rain bread from heaven everyday, as a test as to whether the people would still walk in His instructions.

The Lord urges us to listen to His instructions as one who is in love listens to the whispers of his lover in her ear. He has personal words of instructions for you and me, words that will give us life, words that will give us the power to fulfil what He has commanded and be more fruitful. But sometimes we fail to heed these instructions and end up reaping of our own choices. God has bestowed on us the majesty of choice, but when we reap of its fruits, sometimes, we end up interpreting that as punishment from Him, yet it is a fulfilling of our own will.

Maybe God is challenging you to trust Him and Him alone. Maybe your material possessions and your life accomplishments have created a feeling that you do not need God anymore. Maybe lately you have put your trust in your investments, or in your high profile connections. Sometimes when we have some asset somewhere that brings us money at the end of the month, or some shares that we know we can always count on incase of any eventuality, or it could even be that retirement benefit that you are looking forward to, whatever it is, we rarely recognize that these material things cause us not to depend on God.

You may have pushed God away from your life and no longer honour Him as your partner. God will most of the times take away that which is diverting your trust in Him so as to restore your dependency on Him. Maybe all He wants is for you to say at the end of the day, that even though some may trust in horses, and some trust in chariots, that you, put your trust in the Lord your God. As loving as our heavenly Father is, He sometimes allows us to be brought to our knees by our circumstances, and it is by being on our knees that we are in a position perfect to go to Him for comfort, strength, and solace

Sometimes God allows us to go through pain and suffering so that He can manifest His love over you, because only He can love you unconditionally. When no one is there to help you in your pain, the Lord will be right by your side. He will want to teach you to take refuge under the shadow of His wings. When all your friends get tired of your problems, and your family leaves you, the Lord will stay with you, to comfort you, to strengthen you, to be your refuge. When the storms of life glare at your face, it is the Lord who will give you a heavenly calmness and peace of mind.

A time will come when you will be wrongly accused, and all those who you thought were your friends will betray you. A time will come when you will not know who to trust anymore, when people will look at you with malicious eyes, but the Lord will be there to assure you that it is He who knows your heart better than anyone else, that it is He who can search your heart, and even know your deepest thoughts. He will not fail you no matter what your mind tells. And in all that, He will be preparing you to be a testimony to other people about Him being the friend that sticks closer than a brother. You will have a testimony about a friend that gently prodded with you, closely holding your hand, and lifting you up when your legs were too feeble to walk.

Maybe He is challenging you to return to your first love. To quit running away from Him every time He finds you, which some of us are so good at, sorry to say. You may have become so comfortable in your little pleasures and vices, and that is what is keeping you from what God wants you to be. If there is a battle that God is not prepared to lose, it is turning you into what He wants you to be, and could be trials are His way of bringing you back to His family, making you return to the innocence of your youth. If only we could understand that sometimes the hardships that we go through, the burdens that we bear, all the tests and trials, the heartaches and heartbreaks, the pressures and the squeezes are sometimes steps only meant to take us back to our first love.

Deuteronomy 8:16 - "...humble you and to test you so that in the end it might go well with you"

More often than not when we have everything that we need, when we have enough to eat and drink, when our granaries are full, we tend not to thirst for God, we tend to distance ourselves from our God who created us with a God shaped void in us that only He can fill. So He will from time to time take us to a wilderness where we shall have a season of lack that will help us to recapture our thirst for Him, and bring back the overwhelming desire to be in His presence, and bring us closer to the giver of life, the giver of living water. And it is in your wilderness that the Lord will make a way in the Red Sea, like He did for the children of Israel. God does not intend for you to dwell in your wilderness but to pass through it and go to your promised land. But you have to understand that He leads you through the wilderness so as to humble you.

I can say that what I went through really humbled me and brought me to a understanding of WHO GOD IS, and WHO I AM NOT!! And He brought me to a humbling realization of my ONLY dependence on Him. He stripped me of my arrogance, He stripped me of my pride. If my baby had survived, and I had a life exactly the same way I thought I would have it, there is no way God would have used me, because in that state I was a vessel unfit for His use. I was too strong in myself, and He therefore had to get rid of that 'self' element in me. He had to break me completely back into a moldable state.

Life as it is today causes us to find ourselves disobeying God either through sins of commission or sins of omission. I am reminded of a very powerful story in the bible of a man called Jonah, a prophet who disobeyed God. The bible says that the word of the Lord came to Jonah and commissioned him to go to Nineveh to preach since Nineveh's wickedness was too much.

So Jonah did not really fancy the idea so he plotted to run away (from God, this man was a cartoon of sort!). So he ran away from the Lord and headed to Tarshish. You know the story. So Jonah's mission was very clear, though he did not like it at all. There was absolutely no doubt as to what the Lord expected him to do. It was not even a matter of being indecisive, he knew in his heart what he was supposed to do yet he chose not to do it.

So Jonah as we know boarded a ship to Tarshish, and it was then that the Lord sent a great wind on the sea and such a violent storm arose, thunders roared, lightning flashed, and the waves were so strong that the ship threatened to break up. When the sailors were worrying about the storm, Jonah was deeply sleeping, but he was woken up and when the sailors agreed to cast lots to find out who was responsible for the calamity, the lot fell on Jonah, and when the sea got rougher and rougher, he was thrown out of the ship, "and the Lord provided a great fish to swallow Jonah, and Jonah was inside the fish three days and three nights" Jonah 1:17. It was then that Jonah prayed to God from inside the fish belly, and when the word of the Lord came to him a second time, Jonah obeyed. I can bet that after what Jonah had been through, he came out of that fish belly saying "Here I am Lord, send me, send me!"

There are people reading this book who God has commissioned to penetrate into the core of the enemy's home, some of you have a calling and you know that you know that you know, yet you choose to run away from your calling. Some of you have been called to preach the gospel, but you have looked for every reason not to. Maybe God has appointed you to be His representative at your work place, at your estate, to announce to your friends, relatives and workmates that their wickedness is an offence to God, but you have chosen to deafen your ear to the calling and the commissioning of God. You would rather disobey God than offend your friends. Some of us are ready to pack our bags and go somewhere, anywhere, as far as it will help us escape our calling, as far as it will help us escape our responsibility in the kingdom, but just like Jonah, God will always find a way to bring you back to His calling. The Lord will never give up on you, He will keep trying time and time again to bring you back to your first love for Him, no matter what your strategy of escape is.

My brother, my sister, have you been trying to run away from God, have you been trying to run away from your calling? Have you like Jonah in the ship gone into some sort of false sleep so as to convince yourself that you have actually not done anything wrong against God, telling yourself day in day out that it probably doesn't matter? Maybe just like Jonah you look at how the world responds to the message of the gospel and you have given up on your calling? Are you feeling too inadequate to confront and engage the world? Maybe you feel ineffective in the kingdom, that you are not achieving much in the kingdom and have felt that the best thing to do is to disown the calling?

Like our friend Jonah, God is going to cause such a storm in your life. Your ship will no doubt get thrown about, and tossed in all directions upon the waves. In that world where you have decided to join the rest of the world, the storm will be so strong, but those who will be with you will not care so much about you as they will be busy trying to save their own lives. God will make sure that He will cause such a storm in your life that you will not have any other refuge except in Him. He will want to show you that you cannot run away from Him even in all your wisdom. He wants you to bear fruit for Him even in this stubborn hard headed world. Why don't you make a prayer like Jonah, and the Lord shall surely command whatever fish He has allowed to swallow you, to vomit you back to dry land, away from the storm you are facing today.

John 15:2 - "Every branch in Me that does not bear fruit He takes away; and every branch that bears fruit He prunes, that it may bear more fruit.

God says He will from time to time prune His garden. Even after pruning, a grape will still not be ready to become some sweet wine until it goes through some squeezing! Get ready for some little squeezing if you want God to use you as wine that will benefit others. It is up to you to decide whether you will resist the squeezing or you will yield. He is committed to refining you through the furnace of affliction until you become pure as gold. Unless we experience the refiner's fire, we can never learn the character of God. The same way He used captivity to remove the spirit of rebellion from the Israelites is the same way He will use stressful situations in our lives to remove the spirit of rebellion against Him.

You may not necessarily be doing sinful things that need pruning, but for as long as you are doing something that is propelling you in a direction opposite to that which He wants you in, like Jonah, He will for sure prune you!! If what you are doing is distracting you from God's purpose for your life, then God will sure work His pruning sheers on you, to make you fruitful in that which you are called for, and the sooner you realize this, the shorter your trial period will be. The sooner you drop that victim mentality and adopt a student mentality, the sooner you choose not to waste your trial but to instead turn your pain into gain, the sooner you will rise to another level.

That thorn that you so want removed from your flesh could be the vehicle that the Lord is using to bring to you a message of peace, the kind of peace that transcends all human understanding. That thorn could be a vehicle by which He wants to deliver to you a message of His power. Wait as He teaches you that He is the great I AM. They also bring a message of potential. Things that you previously thought you could never have the strength to go through, He makes you see just how strong you can be in Him. He reveals the potential that He has put in you to do great things, things so great that you could never have imagined yourself doing were it not for the thorn.

Maybe He is preparing you to be of help to those who are going through the same situation. How will you feel their pain unless you yourself have gone through it? Maybe God wants you to be in it a little longer, letting you stay in that situation a little longer, with a divine purpose. His delayed answer may not mean that He has slammed the door on you, He may just have opened the door just wide enough for you to squeeze through it. No matter how big your trial may seem, do not be bowed down in sadness, instead, go on calmly, joyfully and triumphantly, rejoicing in your infirmities, for you know the one who says that His grace is sufficient for you, and knowing that you shall see His glory in the end of it all. March on, knowing that He is teaching you, guiding you, instructing you, and pruning you so that you can become a more fruitful branch of the vine.

God maybe plating that thorn in your flesh so that you can be, and you can have a testimony, because there sure is glory in your story. He wants you to testify of His power to calm storms. He wants you to testify of His person. He wants you to testify that He is God, bringing you to your knees to worship Him as the master of the sea and the storms. And you do not have to wait until the storm is over for you to worship Him, you can do it right in the middle of the storm. Nothing will reveal your faith in His power more than you bowing down to Him right when the winds of life are blowing contrary to you and your boat is about to capsize.

If you remember, at the beginning of my story I narrated my ordeal after I lost my baby. Mine was a case that doctors never understood how I was able to survive the surgery. I still do not know if there is any medical explanation as to why I did not bleed to death considering my blood pressure was so high that doctors did not want me in surgery, though there was no option at that time, given I had bled internally for so long as they tried to induce me to give birth normally in vain. The bible talks about a branch that gets cut, and a branch that gets pruned. That branch that gets cut is the branch that cannot bear fruit at all, and that branch that gets pruned is that which can bear fruit, but isn't bearing much fruit, so it gets pruned so as to bear more fruit. In my interpretation of what happened to me, my work on earth was not done, I was still capable of bearing much fruit, and I choose to believe that is why God could not let the straggly branch (me) to be completely cut, but instead, be pruned to bear more fruit in the kingdom. I can tell you that though I knew the pruning was important, for some time I could not stand Joyce Meyer's messages because I would feel like she was always talking about me; you all know how Joyce likes to talk about pruning.

John 11:4 - "...This sickness is not unto death, but for the glory of God, that the Son of God may be glorified through it"

Remember when Lazarus got very sick and his sisters were very worried when they went up to Jesus. He said everything was for the glory of God. This means that the majesty of God is to be revealed through our weaknesses, through our sicknesses. Lazarus sickness and eventual death acted as an incubator for his greatness. It is through our shortcomings that His power and His greatness are displayed. He chooses our weaknesses so as to show His divinity in our humanity. All you've got to understand is that He makes all circumstances and situations to work together for His own divine purpose so as to produce His glory.

Whatever reason it is, your work is to know that in the end, you will be totally victorious, and through it all, His mercies shall endure forever. No matter how deep in trial you may be, you shall not get outside His mercies . Even when you walk through the valley of the shadow of death, His mercies shall be there. I believe that the Lord Himself shall help you to hold on to that rope of faith until you feel the heavenly whisper reminding you that He is still there, even when you do not see Him, or even feel His presence!! It is during the dark times of trials and tribulations that your faith should go deeper grasping the rock of His promises more firmly, praying and holding on, giving Him a chance to work in you, as you await on Him to come in His glory for your relief.

Hebrews 12:11 - Now no chastening seems to be joyful for the present, but painful; nevertheless, afterward it yields the peaceable fruit of righteousness to those who have been trained by it.

Maybe you have been stuck in one situation for a long time and no matter what you try to do, no matter all your efforts, there seems to be no light at the end of the tunnel. You look at the storm and it seems like it will never end, like there is possibly no good thing that can come from the storm. Just like a diamond, God will have to extract you from the ground, from deep within the earth and smoothen up all the rough edges. He will buff you up and polish you up with His tender loving care until you become that shiny stone that will shine so bright and beautiful for all to see.

Am reminded about the children of Israel when they were passing through the wilderness and there was no water to drink. They became so thirsty that they even wanted to stone Moses to death. Moses smote a rock with his rod and water gushed forth. The wilderness was a place of many trials and temptations, the

Israelites knew how to worship God, but instead they chose to complain, which grieved God. They chose to harden their hearts and to rebel, and at the end God swore that they would not enter His rest. A people who were highly favoured of God, a people who witnessed miracles first hand had chosen not to learn from their experience in the wilderness. After all they had been through, they failed to walk in obedience, thus failing to enter the promised land.

After all that I have been through, I have purposed in my heart that my experiences in my wilderness will not overthrow me, that I will stop hardening my heart, that I will now seek to walk in obedience. I have chosen to see all my experiences as a way that God used to 'circumcise my heart, and the heart of my seed, to love the Lord my God with all my heart, and all my soul, that I may live'.

Maybe it has reached a point where you are now bargaining with God, "God if you remove this thorn from my flesh, I will do this and that for you". But do you know that unanswered prayers are sometimes acts of kindness, so relax, if it is a God-planted thorn, if it is a God-planted storm, don't you dare force it away, because it will rage on until it has accomplished the purpose for which God intended it to. Relax, He may be preparing you for a grand debut in His kingdom! If anything, you should be praying to Him that He prunes you so as to remove the deadwood, and the straggly branches in your life. These deadwood maybe in terms of your sins, your bad habits that may not necessarily be sin but those that cause you not to be fruitful.

Genesis 50:19-20 - "Don't be afraid. Am I in the place of God? You intended to harm me, but God intended it for good to accomplish what is now being done, the saving of many lives."

Pray that He prunes away those friends who are of negative influence in your life making you not reach your full potential in the kingdom. Pray that He prunes even in those areas where you are very productive, so that you can be more productive. In all things, life and death, thank God for shaping you into the person that He wants you to be, and discern to find wisdom and understanding into all the storms that you pass through, that you may see things from God's perspective, "...For as the heavens are higher than the earth, so are my ways higher than your ways, and my thoughts than your thoughts..", says the Lord!

When you wake up tomorrow, remember that most (not all) of what happens in your life relates to His divine sculpting, and that God as your creator and sculptor, continues to sculpt your spirit to be more Christ-like, and He will continue to chip away any portion of the stone that does not seem to take up the appearance of Christ, and one of these day, you are going to emerge a glorious creation worthy of the glorious place He has prepared for us in heaven. As the master strategist, He will continually teach and train you, cultivating you and conforming you into His own image.

Remember when Joseph was sold into slavery and God turned the situation around for his good. So whether a situation is God sent or not, it can be God used, because God will usually breed greatness out of the most painful and the worst situations in our lives!!

SCRIPTURE FOCUS

Jonah 2:1-10

From inside the fish Jonah prayed to the Lord his God.

He said: " In my distress I called to the Lord, and He answered me. From the depths of the grave I called for help, and you listened to my cry.

You hurled me into the deep, into the very heart of the seas, and the currents swirled about me; all your waves and breakers swept over me.

I said, 'I have been banished from your sight, yet I look again towards your holy temple.'

The engulfing waters threatened me, the deep surrounded me; seaweed was wrapped around my head.

To the roots of the mountains I sank down; the earth beneath barred me in for ever. But you brought my life up from the pit, O Lord my God.

When my life was ebbing away, I remembered you, Lord, and my prayer rose to you, to your holy temple.

Those who cling to worthless idols forfeit the grace that could be theirs,

But I, with a song of thanksgiving will sacrifice to you. What I have vowed I will make good. Salvation comes from the Lord"

And the Lord commanded the fish, and it vomited Jonah onto dry Land.

Psalms 121:1-8

I lift my eyes to the hills, where does my help come from?

My help comes from the Lord, the maker of heaven and earth.

He will not let your foot slip, He who watches over you will not slumber;

Indeed, He who watches over Israel will neither slumber nor sleep.

The Lord watches over you, the Lord is your shade at your right hand;

The sun will not harm you by day, nor the moon by night.

The Lord will keep you from all harm, He will watch over your life;

The Lord will watch over your coming and going, both now and forever more.

Chapter 8

Re-Digging My Wells

*T*HE BIBLE IN the book of Genesis 27 tells us the story of Isaac when he left Canaan, his native land where Abraham his father had lived. He went to live with Philistines in a place called Gerar. Here, sometimes the famine would be so great but the Lord commanded Isaac to plant his crops, and He, God, would bless him even in the time of famine. Isaac obeyed God. Because of envy, the Philistines had filled the wells that Abraham had dug so Isaac therefore started re-digging them. Re-digging the wells was not easy as quarrels came up every time he re-dug a well, and he then gave up the wells to them, and moved on to dig other wells.

Just like the Philistines envied Isaac and quarrelled when he re-dug the well, every time the Lord promises to bless you and to multiply you even in times of famines, there will always be people who will not be happy with your success. Some will pretend to be your friends, they will come after you and fill your wells with soil behind your back.

After I had lost my job, I got another job in a flower farm in Ruiru. I thought that I had finally got the chance to re-dig my wells and get my career back. But joining the organization came with its own demons. There were some employees who I found there who probably felt that I did not deserve to be there. They therefore tried from time to time to throw soil back to the wells that I was busy trying to re-dig. I felt that my work was being sabotaged. These frustrations coupled with my deteriorating health (as a result of going to the cold rooms frequently, the flower storage areas where the temperatures were too low, not forgetting that my system had not fully recovered) made me resign, giving up the wells I had dug to my jealous and opportunistic Philistines.

But I knew the Lord was on my side, I did not give up, just as Isaac continued to re-dig the wells and finally found one that gave him fresh water and brought no quarrel, I kept hoping that there was a well somewhere, a well that was my destiny. Since then, I have so far come to a place, where even though it is not my destiny, I can confidently say that it is from here that I can see my very unique destiny in the horizon.

Maybe you have also been trying to re-dig your wells but every time you do, there is a quarrel, there is opposition, and the enemy keeps filling them with soil. No matter how many times he keeps filling your wells with soil, do not give up digging the wells, in the end if the Lord has promised you victory then you will emerge victorious, just hold on and fight through as you re-dig. Do not be discouraged by the prevailing conditions, do not be discouraged by the report on the world economy, do not be discouraged by the report from the World Bank. Know that when the Lord promises to bless you and to make you flourish even in famine, He is not consulting the World Bank report, He is not consulting the ministry of finance, and His economy is not the economy of this world.

Genesis 26:22 And he moved from there and dug another well, and they did not quarrel over it. So he called its name Rehoboth, because he said, "For now the LORD has made room for us, and we shall be fruitful in the land."

Is there a business that you started and along the way faced so much opposition that you opted out? It is time to re-dig your well. Do not allow the enemy to block you from what God has promised you, that He will bless you even in famine that He will take care of you in and out of season. Do not let the enemy fill your wells with soil because it is those wells that will eventually give you fresh water. Try and remember the positive aspects of your past and ask God to show you which wells He would want you to re-dig. It does not matter whether you are re-digging your first or your second well, just don't give up, keep re-digging until you find that well that just like Isaac, you can name Rehoboth, keep re-digging until you find that place where you can declare that surely you will flourish in the land, and when that happens, do like Isaac did, build an altar and worship Him!!

What well in your life has the enemy filled with soil? Is it your career? Your marriage? Your relationship with God? God says it is now time to re-dig your wells.

In my early adulthood years my relationship with God was so good, but when I started attending Saturday classes and working on Sundays I watched as this relationship faded away. The influences of the secular world were too much for someone who was not attending church. I watched as the devil filled my well with soil. It was not long before my prayer life became nonexistent. It was not long before I gave up personal bible study. With time my well was fully covered up, my spiritual walk with Christ was no more.

From there I started living a lukewarm life, a life where I knew that yes there was a God, but I choose not to let Him reign in my life. I lived a life where God did not have much say, I did not give Him a chance to lead me. I did what I pleased when I pleased. The devil made sure to fill my well with soil to a point where I completely forgot that I once had a well. It was after the loss of my baby that I came to a realization that I had to re-dig my well, and revive my relationship with Christ. You do not have to go through a near death experience like I did so that you can start re-digging your wells. Do it now, you may not have a second chance like I did. Do not wait until you have no other option but God, make Him your only source of fresh water. Re-dig that well today, revive your relationship with Him today, and do not let an accident force you to your knees.

Do not make your parents efforts to bring you up in a Godly way futile, do not allow the secular world which we can refer to here as the philistines, to continue filling up wells that were dug by your parents, and your spiritual authorities. Look how as a result, your spiritual gifts have become redundant, and you have piles and piles of unfulfilled promises. Realize that these wells are the source of your water supply, and you cannot continue to watch as the enemy continues to affect the flow of this water, or its quality. Stand up for your generation, stand up for your family, and re-claim the wells that your fore fathers dug. Wake up and revive the spiritual fire that was lit in you ages ago.

What is it that when you look back at your life you find worth recovering? Has your salvation lost its relevance to you now that you have a good job, a nice house, a thriving business? Has bible study lost relevance to you? Have you forsaken the fellowship of believers? I do not want to take you back to your past, but you have got to realize that moving ahead does not necessarily mean getting new things, but it also means holding on to that which was your 'source of fresh water'.

Are you facing a challenge for which you feel the answer lies in what the 21st century economy says? Think twice, maybe the answer is in those wells that your forefathers dug before your time. Maybe there is a family business that you have forsaken because you think it is too ancient, ask yourself if this is one of those wells that you need to re-dig. There are some things in our lives that ought not to be lost.

When I look back into my life, I realize just how wrong I was to let go of some friendships that were a source of 'fresh water'. It takes humility sometimes to re-dig old wells, but I am doing just that. I am claiming back friendships that the enemy had soiled. I am reviving the spiritual fires that were lit up back in my Sunday school days, am reviving the spiritual fires that were lit up in my early youth. I am done with the enemy trying to soil every well that I dig.

SCRIPTURE FOCUS

Genesis 26:17 – 22

So Isaac moved away from there and encamped in the valley of Gerar and settled there.

Isaac re-opened the wells that had been dug in the time of his father Abraham, which the Philistines had stopped up after Abraham died, and he gave them the same names his father had given them.

Isaac's servants dug in the valley and discovered a well of fresh water there.

But the herdsmen of Gerar quarrelled with Isaac's herdsmen and said, "the water is ours!" so he named the well Esek, because they disputed with him

Then they dug another well, but they quarrelled over that also, so he named it Sitnah.

He moved on from there and dug another well, and no one quarrelled over it. He named it Rehoboth, saying, "Now the Lord has given us room and we will flourish in the land"

Chapter 9

A Journey Of Self-Forgiveness & The Resultant Joy

Y EXPERIENCE MADE me realize just how far I had wandered from God, wanting to push Him away from my life. It made me look back and see how much grip the spirit of rebellion had on me. There was a great sense of guilt and shame. No matter how much I tried to shed the guilt and shame away, I always felt like I was beyond forgiveness. I prayed to God to root out the rebel in me, I asked Him to cleanse me from every desire to rebel against Him, but no matter how much I prayed, the weight of my past still brought me down. This made me go on with a burdened heart. I had lost my joy. I was now in a path of self destruction. As much as I knew that God had forgiven me, I found it hard to forgive myself. I was now drowning in sorrow, shame, guilt and self condemnation.

In my mind I kept replaying the mistakes of my past; I kept remembering all the sins of my youth. I kept watering my pillows with bitter tears that seemed to have no end. I was just too harsh on my self, I judged myself mercilessly. It was more like having a grudge with myself. I hated myself so much that I could not find self worth and approval from within and even from God. I tried seeking approval from others . I feared God's temper and judgment, at that time I saw God more as a God of judgment and wrath than a God of compassion, mercy, tenderness, forgiveness, sympathy and love.

My unrealistic way of dealing with my guilt made me deprive myself of happiness. I had cut myself off from joy, I had lost my sense of self worth and every day became a self made nightmare. As though I hadn't suffered enough by losing my baby, I tortured myself with replays of how I had bragged that all I wanted in life was a baby, and had sworn never to get married. I replayed a conversation I had with a friend telling him how I didn't want to go to church because church expected me to have a baby within the institution of marriage. All these replays made me hate myself. I carried a burden of shame wherever I went.

But a time came when I said enough was enough. I had to rescue myself from my view of myself, and see myself from God's eyes. I had to solidify my awareness of my own worth. I decided to forgive myself and to stop causing myself any more torment. I released myself from the feeling of depression and stopped punishing myself when the Lord had already forgiven me. I decided to start afresh, turning on a brand new leaf and vowed to forgive myself completely. It was time for me to stop being harsh on myself and realize that I am a lifetime project, growing each day, progressing each day, a day at a time.

My life is now more exciting, and more purposeful. I now look into His hands and all I see are nail-pierced hands, hands full of forgiveness, and so I learn day by day to extend the same forgiveness to myself. I now have found freedom and peace of mind as I continue to experience His warm love and understanding.

You cannot imagine the impact that learning to forgive myself has brought into my life. I have become more mature, I have learnt to forgive others, even when they have hurt me so much because I now know how hurtful and destructive it can be to live a life where there is no forgiveness. I have learnt to tolerate others. I have now learnt to keep my self esteem at an all time high and I love me so much, after realizing that God wants me to see myself as forgiven, just the way He sees me. I now approach Him more as a father than a judge. My conversations with Him have changed. I can tell Him my dreams and aspirations without having to fear His judgment. I have made Him my best friend, always sharing with Him my enthusiasms.

Shedding off my guilt and lifting the veil of shame has returned me to a place of joy, a joy that I seek to safeguard no matter what the circumstance, a joy that I now want to safeguard no matter what report I hear. I purpose to keep my joy despite what the weather man says. I purpose to keep my joy no matter what the World Bank report or the finance minister says. I purpose to keep my joy no matter what the devil tries to whisper to my ears. Hard as it might be, I try.

Psalm 103:12 - As far as the east is from the west, so far has He removed our transgressions from us.

You may also be going through a season of self blame, burdening yourself with the weight of self condemnation and unforgiveness. You keep reviewing scenes from your past and are very remorseful over what you have done, and are just wishing there was a way you could get a second chance, then you would do it differently this time round. I can encourage you by telling you that the past is just that, the past! And it should not steal your joy from you.

When the Lord looks at you, He does not see your past because He has already forgiven you, and has already covered those sins of the past. The bible tells us that even though your sins as red as scarlet, He is able to make them white as snow, and as far as east is from the west, so far has He removed your sins from you. So learn today to overcome the spirit of remorse.

When God looks at you, He does not look at you with condemnation in His eyes, but with forgiveness and love. He does not remember your sins against you anymore, because He has blotted them out from His remembrance. Try releasing yourself from that burden of self condemnation and you will experience the same kind of joy that I experienced the day I decided to let go of my regrets. You will be overcome with the joy that overcame me the day I forgave myself for running away from God just so I could have my own definition of a family, a family without a father figure (which is against God's plan for mankind).

I have learnt from my mistakes, and the forgiveness that I got from God has really taught me to forgive others. I no longer look at others with eyes of criticalness, but instead I look at others with eyes of love and forgiveness. I have learnt, and I am still learning to silence the critical voices inside me, whether they be against me or against other people.

Nehemiah 8:10 - Then he said to them, "Go your way, eat the fat, drink the sweet, and send portions to those for whom nothing is prepared; for this day is holy to our Lord. Do not sorrow, for the joy of the Lord is your strength."

So you are wondering what this joy is that will result from self forgiveness. I have also had my fair share of trying to understand just how I can be expected to remain joyful in such a chaotic world. Just the other day I was watching on television as a government official addressed villagers telling them they were dying from cholera because they were not observing hygienic standards. As I looked into the villagers faces, their eyes portrayed a lot of pain. It's like they seemed to scream back that they cannot afford water, that their meager earnings cannot even afford them two meals in a day. It is the same every day, our lives are miserable. The economic crisis has only made things worse for most people. Joy is scarce.

And I started thinking back about the day each one of us was born, I am sure there was joy the same way everyone celebrates the arrival of a newborn baby. Every baby is received as a bundle of joy and I thought that then God wants us to remain so for the rest of our lives. But what happens around us does not let us remain joyful, we are a miserable lot. Low wages, high taxation, high cost of living, wars, political instability, violence, calamities all around us which makes joy such a cruel joke. Yet the bible in the book of Isaiah 35 talks about joy. That gladness and joy will overtake us, that in the fullness of God the impossible can happen, that the desert and the parched land will be glad, that the wilderness will rejoice and blossom. This scripture just does not seem to make sense in this age, or does it? How do you tell someone who has not had a meal in three days to stay joyful?

Does that boy who dropped out of school due to lack of school fees have anything to rejoice about? Does that school girl who just got chased away from home for getting pregnant have anything to rejoice about? Does that mother whose husband has run off with a younger girl and left her with four children to look after have anything to be joyful about? And what shall the father whose daughter has been raped and mutilated rejoice over? What shall ones who have lost jobs from the ongoing corporate under sizing all over the world rejoice about? And in this era of HIV &AIDS day, do we expect that young person who has just learnt that she is HIV positve to burst into singing and dance?

The bible says that the devil's mission is to kill, steal and destroy. He is determined to steal your joy, he is determined to kill your hope, he will not rest until he sees you deprived of joy, but we are commanded in John 16:33 to be of good cheer because he has overcome the world, and we too are overcomers. This therefore calls for us not to focus on that which is stealing our joy, but to focus on the victory already found in Jesus. It is a call to stop focusing on earthly things but instead focus on eternal things.

1 Timothy 6:17 - "Command those who are rich in this present age not to be haughty, nor to trust in uncertain riches but in the living God, who gives us richly all things to enjoy."

There is a Jewish saying that best reinforces the idea of being joyful, that "...on the judgement day, a man will be held accountable for every blessing he refused to enjoy." Very well said. No matter how bad times may be, we must not disregard the mercies and the rich bounties that God bestows on us each and every morning. From the scriptures, it is pretty clear that joy is the 'happiness' of spirit, not of the flesh. A happiness that bad circumstances cannot take away, a happiness that lonely nights cannot take away. This is a happiness that will not be diluted by what people think and say about you. It is not a temporal kind of happiness that is determined by your moods or by what you see, feel or touch.

Nehemiah said that joy is the source of all strength, yes, that the joy of the Lord is your strength too. The Lord will give you this strength if you will trade in your own strength, the strength of your flesh, which is weakness in His eyes. You have to realize that you are weak and unhappy in your own human strength until you receive His strength. At that time when you feel that your bones are too tired to carry on, remember that with the joy of the Lord, you will be able to carry on with your day to day activities without having to bury your head in the sand. You will be able to put one foot forward even when all you want to do is just fall off and sleep away.

David, found joy in God's presence offered it back to God as a love gift. In 1st Chronicles 16:27, the bible says at "Splendour and majesty are before Him, strength and joy in His dwelling place" It is only in His presence, His secret place where we have fellowship with Him and receive of Him, that we can tap this joy, a joy that is most abundant and complete. Slipping away to spend time with Him and keeping Him ever present in our minds will give us a heavenly glow, and His aura of joy that will permeate through our circumstances. When we draw close to Him, He fills us with His joy to the overflowing. When we remain in Him, He makes our joy complete.

King Solomon said it is one of the rewards from God for righteous living. When we love the Lord our God with all our hearts, with all our minds, and with all our strength, then He fills us with His joy. He finds greater pleasure in seeing us laugh,

He is delighted when he sees us serving Him while enjoying ourselves. It is in His interest that He sees us happy and enjoying life.

The apostle Paul said it is one of the fruits of the Holy Spirit. When He fills us with His Holy Spirit, then our hearts are no longer empty, we are happy and our hunger is satisfied and can no longer look around in the world for material things that cannot fill the void. When He fills us with the Holy Spirit, then he dwells in us, His dwelling place is in us, and He stays alive in us, and when He stays alive in us, then His joy is ours to experience.

Proverbs 17:22 - A merry heart does good, like medicine, But a broken spirit dries the bones.

Laughter is an outward expression of our joy and happiness. However, laughter and happiness are circumstance based while joy is not. Am talking about that kind of joyfulness that is present even when we are in adverse situations. It is a gift of God, and it comes from the knowledge of what God does for us daily, and what He gives us daily. It comes from looking beyond our pains, suffering and afflictions, and knowing that things will work out for us.

If you think and scrutinize a day in your life, you will realize that more often than not, your joy is not stolen by the big things, rather we lose our joy to small insignificant things in life, like frustrations, interruptions, and inconveniences. It is not always that you lose a family member in death, it is not every day that you lose a job, it is not always that you are sick, yet it is almost everyday that you are not joyful. So what are you losing your joy to? That morning traffic jam that drives you nuts? That *matatu*** tout (conductor) who makes your nerves go haywire? Have you lost your joy just because you cannot find your car keys? Or is it that boss of yours who makes you grumpy all morning?

*matatu - minibus

We all love being around people who are joyful. A happy, joyous face is the first thing that attracts other people towards us. When we are not joyful, we are also depriving our families, our friends, our colleagues the joy that they should also be experiencing. This is because with our joy, which is our strength, we can get to influence those around us positively, but when we lack joy, our influence to others can only be negative. Choose to be a blessing to people brightening up their days wherever you go by being joyful, even "though you have not seen Him, you love Him; and even though you do not see Him now, you believe in Him and are filled with an inexpressible and glorious joy" 1st Peter 1:8.

Sometimes my circumstances dictate that I am gloomy, and yes there is a time for everything, even a time to weep. But when the weeping is over, when the night is passed and the morning is come, there is going to be a special delivery of joy and I will choose to stay joyful. I will choose to see a rose in every thorn, instead of seeing a thorn in every rose. I will choose to react positively to the very small things that steal my joy. I will not allow the small insignificant things in life to ruin my life.

An unknown author once wished someone, "...may you live all the days of your life..." this is just reflective of how some of us do not live though we are alive. We live like we are dead. We have been so favoured of God that He has granted us another day, but then we sleep-walk through life. We fail to enjoy the small miracles of everyday life, we fail to enjoy the sunset, we don't enjoy the rainbow. We don't even enjoy the miracle of life itself. We feel too grown up to jump in the rain. It is so amazing to see the number of tourists that stream into our country just to come and enjoy what God has so freely given to us, that which we ourselves do not enjoy.

Philippians 4:4 - "Rejoice in the Lord always. Again I will say, rejoice!"

Do not lose your sense of gratitude for all the blessings that the good Lord has bestowed on you, do not forget what God has done for you. Instead of whining about your boss, why don't you offer them the best smile and spread some joy? Just look around and you will realise that there is always something to be joyful about, that there always are miracles all around you. Be joyful that the sun rose in the morning, because it means that you have been given a new dawn and a new day to take a few more steps towards your future, and to make a fresh start. Be joyful that the sun set, because it means that you have been given a chance to rest, rejuvenate and renew yourself.

They say you never know what you have until you lose it. Quite true. You never know the beauty of walking until you lose a leg, so enjoy walking. You never know the beauty of singing until you lose your voice, so enjoy singing. God forbid that we should be the kind of people that have to be awoken by life's cruel circumstances just to realize the splendour that lies dormant in our souls.

You may not be in a position to change the weather, but you can sure choose whether it will make you better or bitter. Instead of crying in the pouring rain, you can choose to dance in the rain. Instead of complaining about the cold wind blowing outside, you can instead rejoice that you have a warm jacket.

Tomorrow morning when the sun rises up, I will take notice and smile back to the heavens. When the roses blossom and the rainbow beautifully displays its awesome colours, I will still take notice and rejoice. I am therefore determined to enjoy today, to lead a joy-filled life, and I am determined to give back to the world, and to Jesus, the gift of joy! Have a joyful day!!

SCRIPTURE FOCUS

Nehemiah 8:10

For the joy of the Lord is your strength.

Psalms 16:11

You will show me the path of life: in Your presence is fullness of joy; at Your right hand there

are pleasures for evermore.

Habakkuk 3:17 - 18

Although the fig tree shall not blossom, neither shall fruit be in the vines; the labour of the olive

shall fail, and the fields shall yield no meat; the flock shall be cut off from the fold, and there

shall be no herd in the stalls: Yet I will rejoice in the Lord, I will joy in the God of my

salvation.

Psalms 89: 15 - 18

Blessed is the people that know the joyful sound: they shall walk, 0 Lord, in the light of Your

countenance. In Your name shall they rejoice all the day: and in Your righteousness shall they

be exalted. For You are the glory of their strength: and in Your favour our horn shall be

exalted. For the Lord is our defence; and the Holy One of Israel is our king.

Chapter 10

Learning To Acknowledge Him
Before The Golden Bowl Is Broken

JAMES WAS OUR I.T officer back when I was working for a flower farm, and long after he left, we kept in touch as he would service my home computer from time to time. I was scheduled to meet him but he had just sent a text message saying he was held up in traffic jam and wouldn't make it in time. Since I was already in town and was feeling too tired to run any errands, I decided I might as well sit down and relax as I waited for him. The restaurant was very packed and I could not get an empty table. I figured that by the time James would arrive the place would not be as crowded.

I took a seat near a young lady who was lazily sipping on a soda, she had this far-away look in her eyes, like she wasn't there at all. She just sat there staring into eternity, just staring into nothingness. I decided to interrupt her thoughts by making a comment about the overly loud music in the restaurant. She didn't seem to hear me, but she looked at me as though she had just awoken from a bad dream. "Sorry to impose upon your privacy, but you look very sad", I finally got the courage to talk to her. What followed was an outburst of emotions, crying, sobs that I somehow felt that I had just opened a can of worms.

I didn't want her to attract a lot of attention so I asked her to take a walk with me. We slowly walked out of the restaurant hand in hand as though we had know each a lifetime. As we walked in the street staring into the starry sky, she narrated her story, and I could not help but shed a tear. She had for some time now been in a dejected state of mind. She felt that her life was meaningless, hollow and empty. Of late she had even become suicidal, often contemplating an overdose of clinical drugs. She had just lost the one man that she had devoted her life to since she was a teenager. But this had just turned out to be the start of a series of bad things to come. She later lost her job, and didn't know what to do with her life. She was quickly running out of cash.

This is a story of a girl so successful that her success has intoxicated her into thinking that she cannot be moved. Several paragraphs of this story and I still have not mentioned God anywhere, right? That is because God did not feature anywhere in this young lady's life. She was so inflated with her achievements, so puffed up with her own importance that she did not even give God the slightest credit. She wasn't necessarily a godly person, but she led a good life, a life that didn't necessarily need her to keep praying to God, since she had everything she needed, or so she thought. She had never before given any thought to the fact that God was the supplier of everything that she needed, until now that she had found herself in dire need. She had never thought of God as Jehovah Jireh who supplies our daily bread, who gives us our talents, who gives us the strength to go about our daily chores, the one who gives us happiness. She had always thought or opted to think that she got what she got because she had worked hard for it, or because she deserved and earned it. She never felt that God was right in the middle of it all, and therefore found it irrelevant to be grateful to God for what she had, or even acknowledge His goodness to her over the years, until now.

It is very unfortunate that it would take some people like me and my friend here some really bad and tough times before they can turn to God. Whenever things are going well and life is rosy, they never feel a need for God, but when their boats are threatened by the storms of this life and they are at a point of capsizing, that is the time that they remember that there is a God.

Ecclessiastes 12:6 - "Remember your Creator before the silver cord is loosed, Or the golden bowl is broken, Or the pitcher shattered at the fountain, Or the wheel broken at the well."

Maybe you read this story and see a perfect reflection of your life, a life where you feel you do not need God. You have for a long time felt that you are self sufficient in your career, that you have all the education and experience to make you keep your job, maybe you have for a long time felt that you have all the beauty to keep your husband from being unfaithful to you, right now you could be thinking that yes, you have made enough investments to secure your family's future. Maybe you are one of those people who believe that what you have you got as a matter of right that you are entitled to it. Tell you what? It is said in Ecclesiastes 1:2 "....utterly meaningless! Everything is meaningless.." When what you have has been blown away, what will you be left with? The bible reminds us to remember God "before the silver cord is severed, before the golden bowl is broken" Ecclesiastes 12:6.

There are some among us who have over the years watched as hearses draw up in front of neighbours gates, and watched over the years as sickness and sorrow came over colleagues at the work place. Whenever you watch news on television about the suffering of mankind, there is only a remote connection to what others go through, and can never understand empathy. For a long time you have gone without a pain in your body and cannot even remember the last time you visited a doctor. If you are one of these people, then you must realized how greatly favoured of God you are, and as such must acknowledge Him before the golden bowl is broken!

Ecclesiastes 9:12 - "For man also does not know his time: Like fish taken in a cruel net, Like birds caught in a snare, So the sons of men are snared in an evil time, When it falls suddenly upon them."

Let us not be a generation that remembers God only when things spin out of control, when we fall flat on our faces, let us not be a people that only seek God when we need His healing hand, or when we need His favour to get that so much needed promotion. Let us not be a nation that remembers God only when tribal crashes have broken out in various parts of the country. " As men are caught in a cruel net, or birds are taken in a snare, so men are trapped by evil times, that fall unexpectedly upon them.." Ecclesiastes 9: 12. What will you do my brother, my sister, my friend, when that unexpected time to loose your job comes? What will you fall back on when you lose that family that you so take for granted? Who will you run to when God forbid that you unexpectedly have to hear the cruel words that there is no known cure for your medical condition?

It is very easy to forget God when things are going well in life but the bible says in Proverbs 18:24 says that a man of many companions may come to ruin, but there is a friend who sticks closer than a brother. Maybe you have made your wealth your companion, maybe you have made your health your companion, maybe you have made your career your companion, but a day might come when you may come to ruin, and your friends and family may forsake you. When that day comes, will you have that friend that sticks closer than a brother? A day might come when the wind will shake the tree and cause its figs to fall untimely, what will you do my friend?

I am encouraged by the story of Job. He was a wealthy man who owned several thousand sheep, camels, oxen, donkeys, and even servants, making him one of the wealthiest during his time. But we see him in Job 3:25 saying that what he feared had come upon him, what he dreaded had happened to him. This story teaches us that what we have is not permanent. That is why we are reminded in the book of Deuteronomy 8: 10-18 , that "...When you have eaten and are satisfied, praise the Lord your God for the good land He has given you. Be careful that you do not forget the Lord your God, failing to observe His commands, His laws and His decrees that I am giving you this day. Otherwise, when you eat and are satisfied, when you build fine houses and settle down, and when your herds and flock grow large and your silver and gold increase and all you have is multiplied, then your heart will become proud and you will forget the Lord your God....you may say to yourself, 'my power and the strength of my hands have produced this wealth for me'. But remember the Lord your God, for it is He who gives you the ability to produce wealth, and so confirms His covenant, which He swore to your forefathers, as it is today."

Ecclessiastes12:1 - Remember now your Creator in the days of your youth, before the difficult days come, And the years draw near when you say, "I have no pleasure in them":

Learn to acknowledge God's goodness upon your life today, acknowledge that He is protecting you today, that He is leading you, that He has given you strength to run your business, acknowledge that He has blessed you today with a good job, with good health, with a good family, with good friends. Let Him take His rightful place in your life today, do not revel in your strength of mind and body. Why don't you start your day by proclaiming that this is the day that the Lord has made, and you will rejoice in it and be glad? Why don't you start your day by giving all your worries to God, that way you acknowledge your nothingness without Him, as you focus on His victory over your life. You can never do enough to pay for His goodness towards you, the least that you can do is at least acknowledge Him. Keep on expressing your awareness that He is the one that has brought you thus far, and that He will take you to greater heights.

Learn to see His mighty hand and His awesome love even in the smallest of things in your life. Acknowledge Him for the supply of strength and good health, that He has kept you in safety. Acknowledge Him for His token of love towards you. His eyes have always been upon you since before you were formed in your mother's womb. He has been with you and has watched you each and every step of the way. He hand-picked each and every one of your talent, every gift and characteristic, every fibre of your being was uniquely synchronized so that you may fulfil your purpose on this earth.

It is time that you put God back where He belongs, in the centre of our day to day lives. Acknowledge God for His sovereign power, acknowledge Him for His grace, for His loving kindness, for His great and mighty wonders. Do not forget where you have come from. Why don't you start by making it a habit to tell God 'Thank you' at the end of everyday, 'thank you for seeing me through today, thank you for providing my food today, thank you for my job, thank you that my health is intact, thank you that my family is in one piece, thank you that I have clothes to cover my nakedness'.

Maybe you are reading this and thinking that you probably don't have anything you can thank God for. Well, if by looking around you don't see anything worth thanking Him for, then maybe you could thank Him for what you have escaped so far, thank Him that you have escaped death so far. If you are reading this, you ought to thank Him that you have the gift of sight! And remember, that as you continue acknowledging God for all His blessings, you open the door for more and more blessings to flow in! So why don't you take a pen and paper right now and come up with a 'Gratitude List'? You could start as follows, and you could have so much to write about. By the time you are in the 50th item, you will realize that you are so loved of God.

Gratitude List

I am so grateful to you God because:

I am alive.

I can see.

I can hear.

I can touch.

I can smell.

I can talk.

I can walk.

I can read.

I have a great family.

I have children.

I have a spouse.

I have a job.

Your mercies are new upon me every morning.

My name is engraved on the palm of your hand so that you may not forget me.................... keep going.

SCRIPTURE FOCUS

Ecclesiastes 12:1-3

"Remember now your Creator in the days of your youth, Before the difficult days come, And the years draw near when you say, "I have no pleasure in them":

While the sun and the light, The moon and the stars, Are not darkened, And the clouds do not return after the rain;

In the day when the keepers of the house tremble, And the strong men bow down; When the grinders cease because they are few, and those that look through the windows grow dim..."

Chapter 11

Another Loss And A Lesson In Giving

*T*HE DAY WAS a Sunday and my family had gathered in my house a few months after I lost my baby. My 6-year old niece was unusually quiet that day and she slept on the couch, refused to eat anything or to play with the other kids. We didn't know what was wrong but after several days, several tests, several opinions from doctors in different hospitals, several treatments apparently for her gum, she only got worse.

She had lost 2 teeth but her gum was still bleeding several days after. This is what made the doctors think that she had a gum problem. As she got worse, we were convinced that the gum was not the problem. From Kikuyu Hospital we were sent to Kenyatta National Hospital for a thorough blood test, whose results came after a week. My niece was hospitalized immediately. She had leukaemia, cancer of the blood!

This must have been a nightmare! No one in our family had ever had cancer. This was a first. No, the results must have been wrong, only that they were not. This was a horrible and incomprehensible reality. Cancer had finally reared its ugly head into our family! Nothing could have prepared us for this.

What followed was a painful season of chemotherapy. This small girl was incredibly brave in the face of this cancer and the chemotherapy. I cry for everything she was forced to endure. She fought the most gruelling battle with ease and tolerated so much pain in her body than anyone could even comprehend, and through it all she still kept her smile, her bright spirit never wavered. Her courage and strength awed everyone. Day in day out she got worse and it hurt so much to just watch her suffer and just wait, knowing that we were doing our best and there was nothing else we could do to ease her pain.

During her stay at the hospital I really hated the sound of my phone ringing. The thought of someone calling me and saying that my little niece was no more was more than I could bear.

Biblically our children are not supposed to die before us, it is unnatural. The nightmare pervaded my mind around the clock. I didn't know what to expect then, I had no control over what was going on in my mind. Sleep only seemed to torture me more. I hated myself for loving Eunice because it seemed that God was taking away the people I loved most, and now He wanted to take her too.

I did not know what to do. I wished there was something I could do. I spent my spare time on the internet learning anything I could about cancer. I was reading anything; I was trying to grasp anything that would give me the slightest sliver of hope. I found overwhelming advice, conflicting opinions, until I just gave up the search. I tried my best to be strong for my sister and her family, even though I had no idea what 'strong' meant in a situation like that. Most times I felt that it was my sister who was the strongest of us all. She is one of the strongest women I know. Throughout her daughter's sickness, I never saw her shed a tear in public, I don't know where she used to lock herself and cry, but she never cried in public, such strength!

The chemotherapy was so painful; it ate away the little girl's body slowly. She got so weak as she would sometimes go for weeks without eating forcing her to be confined to her bed since she didn't have the strength to even stand. At some point she developed problems with her leg and had to use a wheel chair for several weeks.

It was too painful for a 6 year old to go through this. Many are the times I asked God why He could not transfer her pain to us grown ups, why He had to let a six year old go through chemotherapy. Compared to the pain I went through, I think Eunice went through it a hundred fold. She was too young to know what she was going through or what she was up against. Sometimes when I listen to grown people whining about their petty problems it makes me sick to the stomach, it makes me want to tell them to visit the children's cancer ward in Kenyatta National Hospital!

In the final leg of her life, Eunice had resumed use of her feet although she was limping slightly. She was so jovial. The doctors had indicated that they were going to release her in the next one week. She was so excited and jumpy. There is a photographer who usually visits the children's cancer ward and every time I visited my niece, she would grab my purse and take away all the coins. She would do this to those visitors she was comfortable with. She would then take photos and pay for them with her collection of coins. She was excited about going home but still wanted to take with her memories of her stay there.

The news of Eunice coming home after so many months in hospital had gotten everyone in a high mood. Her small brother who was so fond of her was so excited that his sister was finally coming home. Eunice's face had an unusual shine and she was looking way too glorious for someone who had gone through chemotherapy. I still look at the last photograph she took and I just can't see a cancer patient in that photo.

A few days before her release from the hospital, Eunice called home and she complained about a stomach ache. The last Saturday I went to see her, she could not eat because her tummy would get an upset immediately after swallowing. Apparently the chemotherapy had killed the cancer cells but eaten away her digestive system. Nurses told us that she used to cry so much in pain. A few days later and Eunice rested. The day she died, nurses said that she had cried the whole morning and she died crying. What hurts me most is that she died alone, with no family member near her, no one to hold her, no one to rub her tummy, no one to even give her a sip of water. Maybe God has a reason why, I don't know. Maybe it would have been too painful for whoever was supposed to visit her that day to watch her die.

That day, I was still very fragile, and emotional from the loss of my own daughter. I still cried a lot from my own pain as I had not gotten over it yet. When I received the news of her passing I was at the AAR clinic in Westlands and I temporarily went out of my mind, I felt a pain so deep and so sharp, as though someone was dragging me with chains down into the darkest of tunnels. I wailed so much I had to be locked in a room as the hospital staff called my boyfriend to come get me.

She was in the hospital for almost a year, during which time as a family we had an arrangement where there would be someone visiting her at the hospital everyday such that there was no single day that she would be alone. I was assigned to visit her on Saturdays. Spending time with Eunice every Saturday taught me how to truly value life, and to give of myself. I gave her all that I could, and it no longer mattered what material things I lacked at that time because to me memories with her was what I was going to be left with in the long run. Because of my tight schedule and my tight budget, I ended up losing very many friends, but it did not matter.

Eunice was with us for only 6 and a half short years but truly her impact will forever be with us. We are forever grateful that she was part of our lives. It has been almost a year today but we constantly think of her. We still cry over what she had to suffer, but the one thing that makes me smile is the dream her grandmother had days before she, Eunice, passed on. In the dream, she was telling her grandmother that she wanted to fly but every time she tried, people, including her brother, would pull her wings down. So she was asking her granny why people did not want her to fly. I am not good at decoding dreams but to me that seemed like a cry from her anguished soul to let her go. That she was going to be fine wherever she was going. Her pain ended, and ours endures.

We do not know how many birthdays we will miss without going nuts over her loss. But what we know is that she is not suffering anymore. I personally have been unable to let go of the photos I have of her in my phone, and just looking at them still spirals me into a frenzy of emotions. Today as I watch my sister, her husband and their boy, I feel so much pain for them. They are such a close family. Eunice meant so much to them and it tears away my heart to look at their photo without Eunice. It has not been easy for them but God's grace has been sufficient, God's grace has kept us from drowning in the sorrow.

Eunice taught me to give unselfishly and cheerfully; completely setting aside my money needs to make her stay at the hospital as comfortable as possible. I had to set aside my social life so as to give her my time every Saturday, to play with her and other children at the hospital. Her sickness taught me that there are bigger things in this world than me, and that I had to get over myself. She taught me to serve others wholeheartedly, all along knowing that I was not in her service, but in the service of the Most High God.

Before everything that has happened happened, I was a giver, but not a cheerful one. I often felt like I was burdening myself while easing things for others who probably needed to work as hard as I was working so that they can stop asking for help. But I now know and appreciate that things happen to people at different time, and that in my abundance I am meant to supply their wants, and in their abundance, they are meant to supply my wants.

These are words from a famous scripture, Luke 6:38, "...Give, and it shall come back to you, a good measure, pressed down, shaken together, and running over, will be poured into your lap, for with the measure you use, it will be measured to you..." Another encouraging scripture is Ecclesiastes 11:1 that tells us to cast our bread upon many waters, for after many days we shall find it again. The principle of sowing and reaping is very biblical. What one sows is what one reaps.

Early in the year 2008 after the chaotic and the 2007 general elections, our nation went through a very trying phase due to the events that occurred as a result of one of the most controversial general elections in the history of our nation. Many of our dear brothers and sisters lost their lives, many lost family members, and properties. Many were rendered homeless. But it was amazing to see how other Kenyans responded with their acts of kindness through giving. Many campaigns were organized to raise food, clothing and money that were all donated to the affected families.

There was such tremendous generosity! Whatever little that people had, they gave. I commend all those who gave not just material items, but those who gave in prayer, those who gave their time to serve others. Truly Kenya is not just a walking nation, it is also a giving nation, and this good will and graciousness make us all proud to be Kenyans.

Have you ever realized that the word GOD is present in the word GOOD? When some good deed is done, God is surely present, and when God is present, and then His power is present. It does not cost us much to give; giving does not have to be done in a heroic scale because even the simplest of good deeds goes a long way. Love begets love. And just a tiny spark of His love, if shown through you and me is able to ignite a great fire in the hearts of others. God wants to use your hands, your feet, your mouth, your finances, He wants to use you to love those who are in need, those who are hurting.

So are you too busy with your daily tasks that you fail to notice that one person who could use a little of your time? Are you too busy to stop, listen and pray for that person who could really use a prayer? If you really have a desire to give, the universe will somehow respond to you in mysterious ways, and make it possible for you to give. Many of us may not have the monetary resources of the rich and wealthy, but we nonetheless have the same opportunities to give. There are people out there who need our encouragement, our time, our guidance, our compassion, our talents, our friendship!

We need to realize that everyone is important, and even if they were the only ones on the face of the earth, Jesus would still have died for them. The Lord Jesus Himself clearly demonstrated how he, as the good shepherd, would leave the ninety nine sheep so as to go back and save the hundredth one, He showed us that He is willing to put aside His shepherding responsibility to go look for the lost sheep.

The Lord is looking for someone who is willing to be a vessel of His love. He is looking for someone who is willing to reach out to those who need some love, those who are confused, those who are in stormy situations and need a little encouragement. He longs to wipe away their tears, He longs to restore their joy, He longs to comfort them, He longs to lift them from their troubles and melt away their confusion and fill their every need. He is asking that you yield your members so that He can use for that. Will you heed His call to let Him use your mouth, your hands, your feet, your smile, your finances? Will you let Him?

Freely you have received, freely give, so says the bible. So why don't you share a little of what God has given you today? Why don't you water others today and witness God watering you? When you take care of others, God takes care of you. The Lord is asking that you be a vessel that pours out to others. He has promised in return that He will never let your well run dry; He shall keep replenishing your barns, your wells, and will continually fill you to overflowing so that you can be a blessing to others.

This is not a time to be consumed by our achievements and our possessions. This is not the time to be selfish and get secluded in what the Lord has blessed us with, no, it is a time look around us and have a heart for those who suffer, those who lack. It is a time to give a drink to that one who is thirsty. It is a time to give food to that one who is hungry. It is a time to say a prayer to those who are perishing in sin, to give a smile and a word of encouragement to that one who is broken hearted. Again, give, and it shall be given unto you, a good measure, pressed down.... and as you reach others, the Lord will reach out to you.

Do not just sit there and say that you have nothing to give, because you have plenty. Just look around you and you will see someone who is overwhelmed, worn down and barely getting by. Your help could be in a form so simple as smiling at them or giving them an encouraging word, without having to even spend a single cent on them. Maybe all that God wants you to do today is to cook someone a simple meal. As you step out and refresh others, remember that the Lord Himself will refresh you in a way that you cannot imagine so go out there and look for that one person that you can bless today.

I like what the revised standard version of 2nd Corinthians 9:8 says " And God is able to provide you with every blessing in abundance, so that you may always have enough of everything and may provide in abundance FOR EVERY GOOD WORK" This verse clearly shows us that our abundance is not just for our own consumption, but also to help others.

Giving is not just an act of kindness, but it is also an act of thanksgiving. When you look at the less fortunate in society, does it not remind you that you have not bribed God to have what you have, that you could as well be in their positions, and therefore trigger a need to just say 'thank you God!' ? It is not because of our righteous acts that we are not in the now famous IDP camps; it is because of God's mercies.

Giving is such a joyful experience, even when you do not have enough yourself. When you visit children's home and you see the bright smiles on those children's faces, it is enough to make you joyful, knowing you have changed someone's life.

I have seen the Lord provide for me when in my most desperate situations. I have seen Him cause people to bless me, sometimes people that I do not know. Believe it today, it is more blessed to give than to receive. Look around you and you will see people that are in need of your help. If you do not see some, then ask God to send you someone who needs your help.

Mid 2008 when I lost my baby and had to be hospitalized for sometime, I needed blood urgently but the hospital only had frozen blood, which could not have been used on me. Fresh warm blood was needed and we did not know where it would come from. My life was at stake but miraculously donors flooded the hospital and I saw God in a manner that was too miraculous to even fathom.

If you ask me, yes, its true, cast your bread upon many waters, for after many days you shall find it again!!

SCRIPTURE FOCUS

Matthew 6:19-21

"Do not store up for yourselves treasures on earth, where moth and rust destroy, and where thieves break in and steal.

But store up for yourselves treasures in heaven, where moth and rust do not destroy, and where thieves do not break in and steal.

For where your treasure is, there your heart will be also."

Luke 6:38

Give, and it will be given to you. A good measure, pressed down, shaken together and running over, will be poured into your lap. For with the measure you use, it will be measured to you."

2Corinthians 9:6-7

Remember this: Whoever sows sparingly will also reap sparingly, and whoever sows generously will also reap generously. Each man should give what he has decided in his heart to give, not reluctantly or under compulsion, for God loves a cheerful giver.

Chapter 12

Being A Prophet Of My Own Life

*L*OSING A FATHER figure, losing a baby, losing a niece, deteriorating health, losing a job, losing property, losing finances, all in one short period! If this is not what you call a dead situation, then I don't know what is. 2008 was a year when almost everything that I valued dried up on me. I started living in a valley of hopelessness, a valley of nothingness. Many were the times I wondered if I could ever come alive again. I wondered if I could ever be restored.

I consistently thought about the story of Ezekiel and how the Lord by the Spirit took him to a valley that was full of bones, and He commanded him to prophesy life into those bones. I meditated on that chapter, and decided I had to do something. I was not going to watch my career and finances dry up, I was not going to just sit and watch as my self esteem dried. I was not going to watch my hope and motivation dry up. I was done being dead spiritually and I was done pity partying over my situation. I was done living in a valley of dry bones.

The past was over, I had to speak over my future. It was time to speak life, it was time to declare, I had to decree, I had to proclaim, I had to pronounce, I had to prophesy!! I had to find my authority in God and soak deep into the Word so that I could get a right standing with God before I could speak His breath into my situation. The bible says in Job 22: 28 that you shall also decide and decree a thing, and it shall be established for you. That means that you are the only one who can stop God from being God in your life. Since I grabbed this truth God has restored me, He has restored my spiritual life, He has restored my career, He has restored my finances, He has breathed life into my very being, given me a new hope, a new faith, and a new vision.

Ezekiel 37:4 - Again He said to me, "Prophesy to these bones, and say to them, 'O dry bones, hear the word of the LORD!

Living in this age of information technology, we find it hard to control our words, but I had made up my mind that I was going to dedicate my mouth to God. We let our words be influenced by the news we hear on TV, we let our words be influenced by what we read on the Internet. In the heat of the moment we sometimes let our emotions dictate our words to us. I know I am very much a victim of this, and I feel so awful when I say something negative because I cannot take it back. We even give the devil too much credit by blaming every bad thing on him yet some of it is our own fault.

Most of us do not realize just how much control we have over our lives. God has been good enough to give us a free will to choose between good and evil. And not only has He given us a free will, but He has also given our tongues the power to prophesy our destinies. What is sad is that we do not realize the power that lies within the words of our mouths, and that what we say today will somehow impact our tomorrow.

I have no doubt you have heard the word of God and deep inside your spirit has said Amen in agreement with God, I have no doubt you have wanted that the promises that God has in store for His children be manifested in your life. Likewise, just like any other human, your mind has tried to convince you otherwise, telling you that you will never be successful, telling you that you will never be healed, telling you that you will remain in poverty. The natural mind has time and time again reminded you that no one has ever made it in your entire extended family. Your mind has been telling you that you will never get married, that just like all the women in your family that your marriage will end in divorce.

Everyday you will be getting reports from everyone, from your friends, from your boss, from your neighbours, from your family, from the media, reports will flood you daily. More often than not, these reports will be contradicting what the Lord says. When those reports come to you, which one will you confess? Will you choose to go by the reports of this world or will you choose to confess the report of the Lord?

You maybe looking back at your life and seeing all the businesses that you have started and none of then have succeeded, they are all dead!! You may be looking back at your life and all you see are opportunities that you have lost. Well, I am writing to tell you that your past is just that, YOUR PAST! The old has gone. Declare new things for yourself, because our God is a God of restoration. Time is now ripe for you to release that kind of mentality, the mentality that tells you that you will never be good enough.

Proverbs 18:21 - Death and life are in the power of the tongue, and those who love it will eat its fruit.

What you allow to come out of your mouth will eventually affect your destiny, whether you like it or not, whether you believe it or not. It will affect your dreams, your vision for the future. It will affect your circumstances and situations. What God is telling you is that you can write your own cheque. That you are the one to determine what life should give you.

In the book of Jeremiah 31:14, the Lord says that His people will be filled with bounty. They will have more than enough. Question is, are you declaring something that is contrary to what God is saying about you? Are you waking up every morning and repeating how you grew up in a poor family and how nobody in your family strikes it rich? Could be for you to really receive what the Lord has in store for you either your tongue will have to be cut off, or you must train your mouth to speak what God speaks about you and your family.

How many times have you spoken things that have acted as stumbling blocks and hindered God's blessings in your life? How many negative words have you spoken over your life that have caused you not to fulfil your destiny? You may not have realized it but you have yourself to blame for some of the negative things that have come along your way. The bible says in Proverbs 12: 18 that reckless words pierce like a sword, but the tongue of the wise brings healing. Your choice of words can either cut your life into tiny painful pieces or they can bring healing to your life.

What will cause us to speak positive things about our future when everything around us is spelling doom? It is the unwavering firm faith and the solid conviction to believe in God despite what other reports say about our lives. It is having to believe God's report without any doubts. And when you believe that positive things will happen in your life, then your mouth begins to speak positive things, and by so doing prophesying your destiny.

We wish and hope for finer things in life, but more often than not we end up speaking against our desires and wishes. We therefore have to synchronize our mouths with God's word. 2nd Corinthians 10:5 tells us to "...demolish every argument and every pretension that sets itself up against the knowledge of God, and we take captive every thought to make it obedient to Christ..." Another version says that we cast down any imagination that exalts itself against the knowledge of God.

Our enemy, the devil will try his best to bombard you with thoughts of doubt, fear, discouragement, hopelessness so as to hinder you from getting what is rightfully yours. When he plants these thoughts into your head, what you do with them will determine your words. You can either dismiss the thoughts or dwell on them. If you chose to dwell on these negative thoughts, you will start having negative imaginations that will later turn into strongholds that will then capture and control your life. If a thought is not in line with God's word, then dismiss it and do not speak them out. It may not be so easy, but we have a weapon, the word of God. If we let our minds be continually renewed, then the devil will not even have a chance to plant negative thoughts in our minds.

Let us not speak idly for we shall be held accountable for every word that we utter. The negative things you say will not only kill you but those who are listening to you too. Are there times when some people have spoken negative words to you and they left you feeling dry and withered? That you even wish they had not spoken to you in the first place? Let your mouth be a vessel of hope to others. Proverbs 15:4 says that a wholesome tongue is a tree of life.

Job 22:28 - You will also declare a thing, and it shall be established.

Your words determine your attitude towards life. They determine the way you feel, the way you act and your whole outlook on life. It is therefore your responsibility to speak forth words to encourage not to discourage, words to heal and not to hurt, words to build up and not to tear down, words to bless and not to curse. If you declare peace, then peace shall be established. If you declare war, then war shall be established.

No matter what fears you see in your path, let your faith see the opposite. Talk faith to your circumstance today. In Numbers chapter 14, the Israelites grumbled against Moses and Aaron as to why they had come out of Egypt only to be in a worse situation. They wished they had died in Egypt. Then we see in verse 28 God telling Moses and Aaron to tell the community these words. "As surely as I live, declares the Lord, I will do to you the very things I heard you say". This is how powerful our words are, that by God doing what He hears us say, the words we say carry the same power as though they came from Him.

With our words we rule our destinies and determine the course of our lives.

In Numbers chapter 13, the people who had been sent to explore the land of Canaan brought the report that Canaan was the land of milk and honey. However, the people they saw were of great size, and they looked like grasshoppers in their own eyes. Only Joshua and Caleb remained confident that they could inherit Canaan and as a result, the whole generation (everyone aged 20 and above) was condemned to die in the wilderness. God swore that out of that generation, only Joshua and Caleb would enter the promised land.

So how do you see yourself today? As a giant or a grasshopper? How you see yourself and speak of yourself will determine whether you will enter your promised land, whether you will achieve your goals and aspirations. There are a so many promises God has given His people in the bible. But we have to keep trusting God and continually speak what is right before Him, no matter how long it takes for Him to fulfil His word.

Romans 12:2 - And do not be conformed to this world, but be transformed by the renewing of your mind, that you may prove what is that good and acceptable and perfect will of God.

Not only should you speak positively but you also have to think positively. There is a call for you to align your thoughts with the word of God and to the thoughts of God. Let your thoughts, desires and attitude be according to the word of God. Let your mind meditate on the word of God even before you can begin to prophesy to your life. The course your mind sets is what your life will follow because your life moves in the path of your most dominating thoughts.

A story is told in the Old Testament, in the book of 1st Samuel 4:19–22 about Eli's daughter-in-law who was about to give birth when news came to her that the Ark of the Covenant had been captured. Her husband had also died in the war. She was so angry that when she delivered a baby boy, she named him *Ichabod*, which meant that "the glory had departed". By so doing she spoke defeat over her son's life and actually, that is the last that we read of this boy as he is not mentioned anywhere else in the bible. In her anger she choose to be negative. Instead, she could have been positive and hopeful and chosen to name the boy "the glory will return".

You may be in a situation where you are tempted to use your current situation to define your future. Speak life and hope to your future even though the present doesn't show any encouraging signs.

Ezekiel 37:9 - Also He said to me, "Prophesy to the breath, prophesy, son of man, and say to the breath, 'Thus says the Lord God: "Come from the four winds, O breath, and breathe on these slain, that they may live."'

Are you feeling as dead as Lazarus. Remember Lazarus? The guy who was already stinking rotten in his tomb? Is your career dead? Is your marriage dead? Is your self-esteem and your self-worth dead? Is your business so dead that it is stinking with loans and overdrafts? Just like Lazarus' sisters, maybe your family and friends think that your situation is too dead. But wait, it is not over until God says it is over! Speak to your deadness, prophesy over your dead bones, and those haters that are laughing at you, and talking about you behind your back, those who thought that you can never make a comeback shall witness you making a glorious comeback into your destiny the same way the crowd witnessed Lazarus coming forth from his tomb!!

Speak what is consistent with God's word, submit your tongue to God and let your words bring life to that dead situation or circumstance that you are going through. Speak words that will set a tone for victory, success, and blessings. Do not utter words that attract defeat and failure. Do not let the words that come out of your mouth bring a curse to yourself and your children. Prophesy healing to your body today, prophesy prosperity in your life, prophesy a promotion in your career, and prophesy a breakthrough in your business. Prophesy peace of mind to yourself. Prophesy life to any dry bones in all aspect of your life today. Call those things that are not, as though they are. Speak faith today because you are a prophet of your own life!!

SCRIPTURE FOCUS

Ezekiel 37: 1-10

The hand of the LORD was upon me, and He brought me out by the Spirit of the LORD and set me down in the middle of the valley; and it was full of bones. 2 He caused me to pass among them round about, and behold, there were very many on the surface of the valley; and lo, they were very dry. He said to me, "Son of man, can these bones live?" And I answered, "O Lord GOD, You know." Again He said to me, "Prophesy over these bones and say to them, 'O dry bones, hear the word of the LORD.' "Thus says the Lord GOD to these bones, 'Behold, I will cause breath to enter you that you may come to life. 'I will put sinews on you, make flesh grow back on you, cover you with skin and put breath in you that you may come alive; and you will know that I am the LORD.'"

So I prophesied as I was commanded; and as I

prophesied, there was a noise, and behold, a rattling; and the bones came together, bone to its bone. And I looked, and behold, sinews were on them, and flesh grew and skin covered them; but there was no breath in them. 9 Then He said to me, "Prophesy to the breath, prophesy, son of man, and say to the breath, 'Thus says the Lord GOD, "Come from the four winds, O breath, and breathe on these slain, that they come to life."'" So I prophesied as He commanded me, and the breath came into them, and they came to life and stood on their feet, an exceedingly great army.

Psalms 141:3

Set a guard over my mouth o Lord; keep watch over the door of my lips.

Proverbs18:21

The tongue has the power of life and death, and those who love it will eat its fruits

Chapter 13

Knowing That His Love Is Certain Even In Uncertain Circumstances

OR SOME TIME I have been questioning some verses in the bible. Just like most of you, I have gone through many ups and downs, mostly downs. But I keep believing in His Word. I keep digging into His Word so as to unearth any hidden promises that I could grab and cling to.

There are too many uncertainties in this life. The world economy is tumbling down, companies are downsizing and people are losing jobs. Relationships are falling apart, marriages are dissolving daily. Nothing seems certain anymore. Nothing seems to last forever. Good health is no longer something that people can boast of because everyone is now living in fear of modern day diseases like cancer, Aids, and heart related ailments. I have learnt that only God is constant!! In this era of Aids, where patients suffer from alienation more than they suffer from the disease itself, God wants you to know that no condition, no disease, will ever break the bond of love that He has with you. He wants you to know that no sickness can ever tarnish it, for it stands stronger than any of these conditions.

There have been times when I have felt lost in familiar places, times when my sense of direction becomes so skewed that I just got confused as to what course of action to take, or what path to follow so as to get back on track. Times that even in my adult life I still wake up and I don't know what I want to be 'when I grow up'. There have been times when I have stared into my mirror and I can not recognize myself. All I wanted was something tangible, some sign board to just show me the way, something to reassure me.

I once got a job that I thought was going to last. But just a few months into the job I started getting sickly, due to the nature of my work. I went to the hospital one too many times until I started questioning God's promise that says that His blessings make rich and add no sorrow. Here I was thinking I finally had the job that was going to take me out of my financial misery and into financial freedom, yet the same blessing was causing me sorrow.

I clung to the word of God, reminding myself that God was faithful, that every word He says is true, that He is a God who does what He says He will do. That He means what He says and He says what He means. That His promises are yes and Amen. Amen is all I needed. That word 'amen' comes from the Greek word '*emet*', which means certainty, firmness, it means stability. I needed stability in my career but I decided I was not going to risk my health anymore. So I quit, it was a hard decision, but I knew that God was in it. I knew that even though my career was very unstable, the love of God was still very stable, and under no circumstances would He withhold His love from me.

Luckily for me, or so I told myself, a certain company had expressed interest in hiring me as a regional marketing manager and we were in the middle of negotiating the package when they realized that I had resigned from my previous job. They decided to adjust the package downwards. I was frustrated, I contemplated rejecting the offer, but in a country where the job market is so flooded, having good papers was not a guarantee that I would get a job soon. I felt all alone, like God had forgotten me. But I knew that though man may lie, 'God is not a man that He should lie', Numbers 23:19. He is not a man that He should change His mind, and that is where my strength came from.

Yes, sometimes we feel like God has forgotten us and even begin doubting His love for us. Our circumstances almost squeeze the life out of us. But God is still God no matter what darkness may loom around us. This means that we can still have confidence in His love for us, and in His word because He is faithful to accomplish whatever good work He has started in us. 1st Thessalonians 5:24 says that 'The one who calls you is faithful and He will do it'. When your world is falling apart, He is faithful to hold you close to His bosom. He is able to kiss away all your pain and heartaches. He is faithful to pour His balm of love upon your fears, your disappointments, your tears, and He is faithful to melt away every single cloud of doubt, of confusion that may be hovering over you. Our God is faithful enough to melt away that bitterness that is holding you from getting your blessings.

There are days when someone asks you how you're doing, and you lie that you are fine, just a little conversational nicety, yet deep inside you are crashing, your very fibre is disintegrating. Deep inside your world is falling apart. At that very moment, chose to leave your situation in the hands of the Almighty, and rest assured that even when you are in the darkest of dark, when the storms are raging and you think you have come to the final bend in the road, that God's love for you will remain. That very moment that you feel that no one cares, and you can hardly find love, when no one seems to understand the hardships and the difficulties that you are going through, that time when you feel that Satan just got permission to swift you as wheat, that is the time to lie back in God's arms and let Him embrace you in His love, let Him give you His certain peace of mind.

Psalms 36:5 - Your mercy, O Lord, is in the heavens; Your faithfulness reaches to the clouds. Your righteousness is like the great mountains; Your judgments are a great deep; O Lord, You preserve man and beast. How precious is Your lovingkindness, O God! Therefore the children of men put their trust under the shadow of Your wings.

There was a time that I would feel so lost and disoriented, and often found myself running to friendships that would somehow create a safe neighbourhood in which I could find comfort, solace, company, but I later realized that even these 'safe neighbourhoods' are not as certain, they only give us sympathy and empathy but cannot guarantee us certain love in uncertain circumstances.

Many are times that our own friends are only willing to listen to us for a period, after which they slowly walk away from us. When mourning the death of my baby, it reached a point where friends began to drift away, and to withdraw their support. Some lapsed into silence whenever I felt like talking about how I felt. These friendships were just too uncertain. I went through a long season when it was so hard to find companionship, with everyone else busy at work and I alone at home, healing. But through it all I made God my best friend as I grew closer and closer to Him every day. Sure I could not see Him or even feel Him, but I knew His love for me was always there, all the time.

I have now learnt to remind myself that even though friends may come into my life, I must continue to focus on the one who gives me certain love in uncertain circumstances, love unconditional. Times change, seasons change, people do change, but the Lord is the same yesterday, today and forever.

Maybe you are locked up in your room wondering and waiting. Wondering when all this is going come to an end, wondering if God really hears your prayers, wondering when the sun is going to shine on you. Well, as the song goes, 'he never said there will always be sunshine, He never said there will be no rain, He only promised a heart full of singing', so as you wait on Him, remember that His love for you is certain, it is stable, and will remain unchanged by your circumstance. When no one else can understand the depth of your despair, when not even your spouse can see the depth of your desperation, when your family members cannot see the depth of your disappointment, God is able to see, and even feel your pain.

Man's Love Is Uncertain

Shortly after I lost my baby, the baby's father who I had long fallen apart with started sending me very heart breaking text messages. My baby's death had sort of given him a leeway to get back at me after I refused to get married to him. When I was still mourning he threatened me that he would make sure I never got a baby with another man! He claimed that he always suspected that since I hated him, I also hated his baby and even accused me of procuring an abortion. This was a man that I once loved enough to change my mind about men and even enough to have a baby with. And here he was causing me untold suffering yet he knew very well that my baby had died as a result of an accident.

I remembered the day he first sent me that text message, I lost all bodily strength, I could not move. I called my mother and cried on phone endlessly. This was more than I could bear. I wished my baby's father could see the depth of my loss, I wished he could see my pain and my despair. During this trying moment, I drew my strength from knowing that Jesus knew and understood the depth of my loss, and the pain of being insulted and wrongly accused by the one person who should have stuck with me through the loss of our baby.

I went through a lot of agony, insult after insult. It was so bad that whenever I refused to pick his calls he would call my mother just to talk nasty at my family. And when my mother refused to pick his calls, he then switched to calling my best friend. He was so determined to hurt me that when I temporarily changed my phone number he had the guts to call my friends mum and lie to her that he was my brother and he was unable to reach me just so that she could give him my new telephone number. How could a man who once loved me so much do this to me? How could a man whose baby I had carried for close to nine months do this to me?

I kept asking God to take the cup of suffering away from me, since He too knew too well how it felt to be abandoned and forsaken by those who loved Him. I echoed the same words He said to His Father at Calvary, "My God! My God! Why have you forsaken me?" when the nails pierced through His hands and feet. And just as Judas has betrayed Him, I too felt betrayed, and I found no certain place to take refuge than in His certain love only. For sure, man's love for another is uncertain, but God's love is certain.

I often felt so low, so weak, and lost for words just to express the pain I was going through. Behind my plastic smile was a helplessness of not knowing how to express the deepest secrets of my hurting heart. But it was in His certain love that I found refuge, a love so unconditional that my finite mind can never fathom. If it wasn't for His love I do not know how I would have made it, I would never have! It was His certain love for me that gave me strength to face the future, it was His certain love for me that renewed my will to live, it was His certain love that saw me through one of the most uncertain phase in my life. He will not forget, falter or fail you. He is love Himself, He says that He loves you unconditionally, He loves you with unending love. A love that flows abundantly but never runs dry, a love that is never used up or lost. Choose to believe that today even though the circumstance around you seems to suggest otherwise. Whose report will you believe? The report from your circumstance or the report from your God? Believe Him today, believe in His love, for every word that comes out of His mouth, an 'Amen' follows it.

If all your situation or circumstance is doing is scream out more negative reports to you, why don't you try scream back to the situation, quoting God's faithful love to you, quoting God's faithful promises to you. Speak to your situation, speak to those dry bones and call them back to life. Do not be ashamed of proclaiming God's love on the dashboard of your car. Do not think it is useless to tell your friends about God's love for you. Refuse to be moved by your circumstance because God's love for you will not be moved.

Romans 8:35 - "Who shall separate us from the love of Christ?" shall tribulation? No! Shall joblessness? No! Shall sickness? No! Shall infirmities? No! Shall anguish? No! Shall famine? No! Shall childlessness? No!

Even when you have failures, and feel like a total disappointment to yourself, to your family, to your friends, and even to God, always remember that though this may cause God to weep for you, to long to help you back into His fold, they do not lessen His love for you, He continues loving you just the same. Those things that you feel bad about, those things that you wish you could change do not make His love any less. Nothing you do could be so bad as to cause Him to love you less. He can never despise you and never will you slip out of His presence. His heart may continually weep over you as a lost child, but never at any time will you be lost to His love.

He is a God who loves the unlovely and those who are difficult to love. His love is one that knows no limits, and goes to any length, even to giving His own Son for us. His love is one that goes to any agony, and walks through any kind of storm with you just to bring you that victory that your battered soul so much desire.

Whenever He looks at you, He does not look at your past, He does not look at your weaknesses and your shortcomings, or your blemishes, He looks at you, His child, His creation. Whenever He looks at you, He sees a diamond in the rough and is only so willing to bring out the jewel in you. From the beginning He loved you, He loves you now, and will continue to do so unconditionally with a love that never grows weary, a love that lives to awaken your spirit, and give you strength to carry on.

It was His unconditional love that saw me as a diamond in the rough and smoothed away the rough edges, polishing me until I can now shine beautifully for all to see. It has been His unconditional love that kept me strong when I was struggling, when I was lost and when I was in total confusion over what I was going through. It has been His unconditional love that has walked with me through the storms.

SCRIPTURE FOCUS

Romans 8: 35 - 39

Who shall separate us from the love of Christ? Shall trouble or hardship or persecution or famine or nakedness or danger or sword? As it is written: "For your sake we face death all day long; we are considered as sheep to be slaughtered." No, in all these things we are more than conquerors through Him who loved us. For I am convinced that neither death nor life, neither angels nor demons, neither the present nor the future, nor any powers, neither height nor depth, nor anything else in all creation, will be able to separate us from the love of God that is in Christ Jesus our Lord.

Psalms 36: 5

Your love, O LORD, reaches to the heavens, your faithfulness to the skies

Psalms 36:7

How priceless is your unfailing love! Both high and low among men find refuge in the shadow of your wings

Psalms 48:9

Within your temple, O God, we meditate on your unfailing love

Psalms 86: 15

But you, O Lord, are a compassionate and gracious God, slow to anger, abounding in love and faithfulness

Psalms 136: 26

Give thanks to the God of heaven. His love endures forever

John 3: 16

For God so loved the world that He gave His one and only Son, that whoever believes in Him shall not perish but have eternal life

Chapter 14

Experiencing His Sufficient Grace

$\mathscr{T}$HE OTHER DAY I was doing my monthly budget and I was amazed to discover just how much we are made to pay for everything that we use (and don't use) under the sun. Gone are the good old days when life was simple. In today's world, even in the simplest of villages, we have to pay for almost everything. From electricity, to water, to rent, to food, we even pay to talk! We have to pay to sustain our friendship and reputation. Nothing comes for free anymore.

It has become such a hard life that even when someone offers something for free, the first question we ordinarily ask is 'what's the catch?', because we are not used to unmerited favours. It has become a 'give-me-that-I-give-you-this' world. We live in a world which has given us a 'you-get-what-you deserve' mentality, implying that what we have is as a result of our own efforts and hard work. We work so hard day in day out to earn material things that we think the same efforts can earn us God's grace.

But it is not so with God's grace. God's power is available for us, to meet our needs even without us having to earn it through our own efforts, but simply by believing it. This is the grace of God! The power without which we can do nothing. The favour of God upon us, that gives us blessings not because we prayed hard, or sang the loudest, or because we read the bible more often and are better than anyone else, no, the un-earned favour of God! Look at how He has provided for us even when we have been downright unfaithful to Him, and awful. Look at how He provided manna to the children of Israel despite their whining and faithlessness in the desert when travelling to the promised land.

The Mystery of Grace

Grace has been defined as the undeserved, unearned, and unmerited favour of God in our lives. It is because of this undeserved favour that Christ died for me on the cross, offering me forgiveness when what I deserved was punishment for my sins, a grace that has pardoned my past and secured my future. It is because of this unmerited favour that I woke up this morning. I did not pay a single dime to deserve to be alive, but because of God's grace upon me, here I am proclaiming His goodness to all nations. I did not earn His mercies that are new upon me this morning and every other morning of my life.

And it is this grace that teaches me to approach our heavenly Father just as I am, with nothing! Not with my accomplishments, not with my works, not with my reputation, not with my titles, not with my education, but with a humble heart and a broken spirit because I have come to learn that the grace of God always succeeds even when works fail. I have come to appreciate that in life when everything seems to be going wrong, what I need most is not to try harder, but to rely on God's grace.

It is also this grace that has taught me to fully trust God, and to die to all dependence on myself. The same way that God humbled Saul (later called Paul), a self proclaimed chief of sinners, once a man who stood high in public favour, who finally found sufficient grace in the Lord, it is the same way that our self righteous souls ought to be humbled so that we can never doubt God's grace. It was to Paul that Jesus said that His grace would be sufficient for him, assuring him that though the burden of the church lay on him, God's grace was going to suffice His trials, His tribulations, His weaknesses, His battles, His needs, His responsibilities, and God's strength was going to be made perfect in weakness.

This sovereign grace has truly humbled me and filled me with thankfulness. Knowing that I have no rights but instead, all I deserve is punishment from Him, a holy and justified fury. It is for this reason that Jesus came, that He may show me mercy. He absorbed God's wrath so where I deserved to die, He gave me life, where there was no hope, He gave me hope. I now have the assurance that He will keep me to the end.

2Corinthians 12:9 - And He said to me, "My grace is sufficient for you, for My strength is made perfect in weakness." Therefore most gladly I will rather boast in my infirmities, that the power of Christ may rest upon me.

It is time, my dear friend, that you realized that your good works, your education, your good reputation, may not be as powerful until you learn to plug into that divine power of God - His grace. Let not the devil deceive you into thinking that you can earn God's grace. God's grace has never been for sale. It is not and will never it be traded for any merit. Do not let your ego deceive you that you can work hard so as to earn His grace because one day your body will grow weary, your flesh will fizzle out, and all you will have left is His grace. So chose today to learn to marvel at this amazing grace.

Likewise, do not let the devil deceive you into thinking that you are not good enough for God's favour. His grace is sufficient even to the person who feels like such a big sinner. Just come to Him and believe and His grace shall be made sufficient for you too. It will enable you live an honourable Christian life. The bible says that in His grace and favour, God chooses the weak and foolish things of this world so as to confound the wise. You can receive His grace just as you are. All you need is to be available to receive it and to be humble enough to realize that it is not by might, nor by power, but by the Spirit of God. So learn to respond to His grace, live by His mercy.

And when you are at it, learn to extend the same grace that God extends to you to all around you. When someone wrongs you, resist the urge to 'return the favour', but instead extend God's grace to them. Why? Because we also do not deserve His grace, but He extends it to us anyway. Let there be an overflow of grace in your life. Be kind to those who do not deserve kindness. Be forgiving to those who do not deserve forgiveness. Love the unlovable.

How encouraging it is to know that no problem is too big for His grace, how reassuring to know that His grace is sufficient for us. Even in the hardest of times, in the worst of economies, His grace shall be sufficient to meet all our needs. It calms my mind to know that when am walking in darkness, and cannot seem to see a glimpse of hope, that His grace shall be sufficient for me each step of the way, and this divine power shall illuminate my path through life's challenges.

Being a child of God or knowing God does not exempt us from going through hard and difficult times. God has not promised to keep His children immune to trouble, so to speak, but what He has promised is that He will be with His children in times of trouble. When an earthquake occurs, it does not discriminate, it kills everyone. When a suicide bomber bombs an aeroplane, everyone in the plane perishes. Our loved ones get terminal illnesses. Rightly or wrongly, we all find ourselves in situations whereby only the grace of God can get us through. We all find ourselves in circumstances that make us sing out aloud, "*Kama si wewe Bwana, ningekuwa wapi? Kama si wewe Bwana ningeitwa nani? Kama si wewe Yesu ningekuwa nani?*" (If it wasn't for you Lord where would I be? If it wasn't for you Lord what would they call me? If it wasn't for you Jesus who would I be?)

God has been so gracious to us that we wonder just like David, what is man that God is so mindful of him?

They say that there is always a new devil for every level, but I have also learnt that it is true that there is sufficient grace for every level! The other day I asked my friend how he copes being in a full time job, having another weekend job, being an online pastor, being a husband and a father, and he told me, "there is grace for every level." As you go along in your daily endeavours, remember, the grace of God is receivable, but it is not sellable!

SCRIPTURE FOCUS

2nd Corinthians 12: 9

My grace is sufficient for you, for my power is made perfect in weakness"

John 1: 16

From the fullness of His grace, we have received one blessing after another.

Zechariah 12: 10

And I will pour out upon the house of David and upon the inhabitants of Jerusalem, the Spirit of grace (or unmerited favour) and supplication.

Chapter 15

Praising My Way To His Presence

*O*VER THE YEARS, I have always found it so automatic to praise God whenever I got a new job, when I have received some good news from a doctor, or when something really nice has happened to me. But what is our motive behind praising. Why and when do we sing praises? Only when we are happy and everything is going our way? Only if we have good voices? Well, the Lord does not only listen to the melodies of our mouths but He also listens to the songs of our hearts. The bible teaches us that if we are in tune with heaven then we should always have a song of praise in our hearts. Always! Even when we are suffering affliction. Even when the harvest is not plentiful, even when friends are few, and yes, even when your family members disown you.

It was really difficult for me to praise when I lost my baby. I tried hard to cover up my feelings of depression and isolation. People would tell me to praise God that at least I was alive, but that was a time when no words of comfort would make any sense to me. I was going through great grief and was stuck in my anger towards God. There was a lot of bitterness in my heart towards God, just like in the case of the Israelites when their drinking water became bitter at a place called Marah. In my Marah-like situation, praise was hard to come by but I knew that the only gate to His presence was through praise. His intervention would only come to me if I entered His gates with thanksgiving and His courts with praise.

I found it hard to see any blessings in my life worth praising the Lord for. I struggled with God for sometime, but there came a time when I had to take the first step and start thanking God even for the very small and most overlooked things in my life. I chose to praise God anyway no matter what I was going through, I chose to constantly have a song of praise on my lips. I found out that with praise, feelings of doubt, feelings of fears and worries were cast away, and as I got deeper and deeper in praise, and in worship, that I became stronger and stronger.

That is when my healing started. I soon found myself praising God for the gift of life, I praised Him for the fact that I lived to tell of His goodness, I praised Him that I have a family that loves me, friends that care about me. I started praising Him that I could see, hear, smell, taste. Soon there was an overflow of praise from my heart. In fact, I no longer needed to have a reason to praise Him. I would praise Him for the simple reason that He is God, for the simple reason that He is the creator.

The bible in 1st Thessalonians 5:16-18 tells us to be joyful always, to pray continually, and to give thanks in all circumstances, for this is God's will in Christ Jesus. The Psalmist in Psalms 34:1 says " I will bless the Lord at ALL times; His praise shall continually be in my mouth. My soul shall make her boast in the Lord; the humble shall hear thereof, and be glad. O magnify the Lord with me, and let us exalt His name together." What secret did these men of old know?

Paul and Silas chose to sing praises when they had been falsely accused, beaten, shouted at, dragged and thrown into prison. It was dark in the prison, they had been chained and their bodies were very sore. Their arms must have been cramped and their feet immobile. Imagine a prison situation where the sanitation is so poor, a stench-ridden dungeon where the atmosphere is very depressing. But instead of singing "oh poor me' songs, they made a conscious decision to sing glorious praises to God. Acts 16: 25-30. When the other prisoners expected to hear their cries, and probably some cursing, they instead were shocked to hear them praising. It is no wonder that their praises caused a mighty release of power from the heavens.

Psalms 40:3 - "...He put a new song in my mouth, a song of praise to our God..."

One need not stretch their thoughts far as to why we should always have a song of praise in our mouths. We were created to praise God and so praising is an act of obedience. When the bible says that from the rising of the sun to the going down of the same, that the name of the Lord is to be praised, it is giving a command, not a suggestion.

To praise means to magnify, to applaud, or to proclaim. We are constantly reminded to proclaim His goodness. To proclaim means to list in detail, it means to speak out, and speaking out loudly so that others can hear. It may not make sense to praise God when going through a hard situation, but it made sense to Paul and Silas. Why? Because they understood what God can do through praises. God already has a way out for us, and our praises can just be a trigger that will open the way for His mighty works. Praising God elevates us into His joyous presence and triggers a release of His awesome power. It is said that what you appreciate appreciates, so if you appreciate God, He appreciates in your life. In a businessman's language, to appreciate means to go higher in value.

Psalms 34:1- I will bless the LORD at all times; His praise shall continually be in my mouth.

There is a very powerful story that I hold dear to me, the story of a potter and the clay, the pottery. The potters of old were not as technologically advanced as the potters of today. They did not have the machinery to show when the pottery was finished, rather when the pottery was burnt to completion. For this reason they used their ears to know if to keep the pottery some more minutes in the fire or to remove it. Why so? Because when the pottery would reach the proper heat point, it would produce a 'singing' sound, and whenever the potter heard the 'singing' sound, he would know that it was time to remove the pottery from the furnace. Note that the pottery would have to sing in the furnace! Today I choose to sing in the furnace of affliction, I chose to sing in the furnace of disease, I chose to sing in the furnace of lack. Oh, I chose to sing in the furnace of joblessness, I chose to lift up my voice in the furnace of a bad economy!

I now know what the men of old knew, that God inhabits the praises of His people, His presence dwells in the praises of His people. If this be the case, the question therefore is how much of a dwelling do I want God to have in my life? The amount of praise I offer Him will therefore determine this. I have therefore made a sober decision to praise anyway, anyhow, no matter what am going through, I will let no one shut me up. So today I choose to belong to the generation that praises God, I choose to proclaim His good deeds to everyone.

David was a Psalmist who praised God in good and in bad times, despite the fact that he spent most of his time in the desert tending his father's sheep. It was in the desert that he most probably composed most of the psalms in the bible. When he wrote the Psalms he had no idea that one day he would be a king, he did not wait to be a king to praise God! He praised God in the desert, he praised God when he had nothing, and the Lord exalted him.

Just like David, my praise is not going to be conditional, I will praise Him when the sun is shining, and when the skies are blue. I will praise Him on the mountain top and in the valley. I wish to let everyone know that "...I was young and now am old, and I have never seen the righteous forsaken..."

Psalms 22:3 But You are holy, enthroned in the praises of Israel.

My God finds great pleasure in the praises of His children. He finds great joy in the praise of His bride. And when we begin to praise Him for His provision and supply, when we begin to exalt Him for His blessings and His protection, His guidance and His instructions, then He will open up the heavens for us.

Maybe you are reading this and wondering how to praise Him, maybe you do not know the words to use. Why not thank Him that His love for you is a free gift and you do not have to earn it. Why not thank Him because He is so understanding and so comforting, that He is always there to reassure you that everything will be well? Lift your hands and thank Him because He always gives you strength, that even as you wait upon Him, He continually renews your strength! Lift your voice and thank Him because your name is engraved on the palm of His hand that He may not forget you! Thank Him because although a mother may forget her young one, He will never forget you!

I was reading the famous A – Z praise poem, and I challenged myself to come up with my own original A – Z praise list. By the time I was in the Z word, I was deeply overwhelmed by guilt seeing how much we need to praise God, and how little we do it. Here is my A – Z praise list.

A – AWESOME:

God is an awesome God. Just look around you, see His creation, breath taking sights to behold, and you will be filled with awe for Him.

B – BLOOD:

Were it not for the blood that was shed on Calvary, I would still be in captivity, I would still be a sinner with no hope of redemption.

C – CREATOR:

He is my creator, your creator, and the creator of all things. He is the mastermind behind the beautiful mountains, the rivers, the valleys, the flowers, the snow, and the forests.

D – DELIVERANCE:

From my personal story, God delivered me from the jaws of death. Death beckoned me, but God with His deliverance came through for me.

E – EVERLASTING:

That He is the same yesterday, today and tomorrow is something worth praising Him for. Knowing that He is the same God who made way for the Israelites in the desert and that He can do that for me today!

F – FORGIVENESS:

If it wasn't for His forgiveness, I would have died a long time ago. But He patiently and lovingly forgives me of my wrongs and makes me whole again.

G – GUARDIAN:

He has been my guardian, commanding His angels concerning me to guard me that I may not strike my foot against a stone.

H – HEALING:

It is by His stripes that I am now healed, it is by His stripes that I am alive and telling my story. He is my healer.

I –IMMANUEL

God with us. Even in times when I have left Him, He continued to be God with me.

J – JIREH

He has been Jehovah Jireh, my provider. And He shall continue to supply all my needs according to His riches in glory by Christ Jesus.

K – KING:

It is because of His kingship that He has been able to calm the storm in my life. It is because of His kingship that He has been able to command goodness and mercy to follow me all the days of my life.

L – LOVE:

His unconditional love for me knows no limit, it knows no stopping place. He loved me when I was unlovable, he loved me when I felt rejected, lost, confused, alone and hurting.

M – MERCIES:

His mercies have been new upon me every morning. His mercies have been a precious gem and my life is rooted on His mercies. Were it not for His mercies, He would not have sent His son to die for my sins.

N – NISSI

He has fought the battle on my behalf and conquered. In my battles of sicknesses, lack, depression, self condemnation, He has fought for me and made me a winner in Him, He is Jehovah my banner.

O – OASIS

In a dry and weary land, He has remained my oasis, my source of fresh water. An oasis that never runs dry, an oasis that never gets diluted.

P – PEACE:

He has given me so much peace of mind. In times of deep turmoil, in times when I almost had a nervous breakdown because of what was happening around me, He gave me peace, a peace that surpasses human understanding.

Q – QUICK TO FORGIVE

Were it not for Him being quick to forgive and to embrace me, were it not for Him being slow to anger, I would have perished way back.

R – RESTORATION:

God has restored me back to Himself, He has restored my health, He has restored my purpose in life, He has restored my joy and peace, He has restored my family, and I am believing in Him to restore much much more.

S – SALVATION:

As a sinner, it was impossible for me to go to God by myself, but God through by His grace, and through the death of His Son Jesus Christ, I now have salvation.

T – TRUTH:

He has shown and taught me the truth through His word, and His truth has set me free.

U – UNCHANGING

He is the same yesterday, today and forever. He is an unchanging God. He has often opened a way for me where there seemed to be no way just like he parted the sea and made a way for the Israelites.

V – VICTORY:

He has given me victory. Though I went through the valley of death, though I went through high seas, He has made me victorious.

W – WORD:

His Word has been a lamp unto my feet and a light unto my path. He has spoken to me through His word, He has molded me through His word, and made me the person He wants me to be.

X – EXALT

He is forever exalted in my life. I have given Him a permanent habitation in my life - at the top most of my highest praise.

Y – YAHWEH

Yahweh is His name. I AM WHO I AM

Z – ZION

He has made me a daughter of Zion, for He has put His words into my mouth, covered me under His shadow, and told me that I am His. Now Zion awaits me.

Somebody help me praise my God because He watches my every move, He knows all my fears, He sees all my tears, He feels all my frustrations, He hears my prayers, He knows my thoughts, He knows all my problems, my burdens and my shortcomings. Somebody help me praise Him because He lifts me from deep pits of despair and cheers up my heart. Somebody help me praise Him because He continually renews my strength, He continually gives me fresh courage, oh, and He gives me renewed vision and an enlightened mind.

I need someone to help me exalt Him above my family, my friends, my career, my business. Oh somebody help me exalt my God high above my problems, high above my circumstances, high above my achievements.

Who will help me praise Him for He is a God whose mercies are new upon me every morning? Who will help me praise this God who is full of love and forgiveness, sympathy, and whose judgement is completely honest? A God who rewards my righteousness, a God who rewards my sacrifices?

SCRIPTURE FOCUS

Psalms 95:1 - 3

"O Come, let us sing unto the Lord: let us make a joyful noise to the rock of our salvation. Let us come before His presence with thanksgiving, and make a joyful noise unto Him with psalms. For the Lord is a great God, and a great King above all gods"

Psalms 96: 1 - 4

"O sing unto the Lord a new song: sing unto the Lord, all the earth. Sing unto the Lord, bless His name; show forth His salvation from day to day. Declare His glory among the heathen, His wonders among all people. For the Lord is great, and greatly to be praised: He is to be feared above all gods"

Psalms 150: 6

"Let everything that hath breath praise the Lord. Praise ye the Lord"

Ephesians 5: 18 - 20

"And be not drunk with wine, wherein is excess; but be filled with the Spirit; Speaking to yourselves in psalms and hymns and spiritual songs, singing and making melody in your heart to the Lord; Giving thanks always for all things unto God the Father in the name of our Lord Jesus Christ;"

Chapter 16

Claiming His Power-filled Promises

*I*F IT WASN'T for God's promises, I do not know if I would have had the strength to go through what I have gone through. If it wasn't for His promise that He will never leave me nor forsake me, I would have lost hope a long time ago. 1st Kings 8:56 tells me that "Not one word has failed of all His good promises". This verse is what has been my strength all along, knowing that everything He has promised me will come to pass, the physical, emotional and spiritual healing, and the restoration, everything He has promised!

It was not enough that I had to read the Word and remind myself of what God has promised me. It was also of utmost necessity that I make these promises very personal and then claim them. I remember a few weeks after losing my baby, my job and my property, I cried so much to God and I reminded God that He promised in Isaiah 43: 2 that when I pass through the waters, He will be with me; and when I pass through the rivers, they will not sweep over me. When I walk through the fire, I will not be burned; the flames will not set me ablaze and just like Shadrack, Meshack and Abednego, I told Him I wanted to come out of this fiery furnace not burnt, and not with the slightest smell of smoke. I told Him that at the end of it all, I wanted His glory visible on my face.

Whenever I felt that I was going through the deepest valley, I reminded myself of Isaiah 55:11 which says that His word, the word that goes out of His mouth, will not return to Him empty, but must accomplish what He desires and achieve the purpose for which He sent it. I remember refusing to sleep because I was so afraid I would die in my sleep, but I would remember His promise in Jeremiah that He had good plans for me, and I told myself dying young was not in His list of good plans.

God gave the Israelites a miraculous deliverance, and even though the wilderness was harsh, He did not leave them at all, if anything, it was the Israelites who kept forsaking God. Same way, He had not saved me from the jaws of death only for Him to leave me alone now.

We Live in a World of Broken Promises

Every time you switch on your television set or your radio, we are saddened by what we see and hear. There are problems everywhere we turn, hopelessness. There is not a week that goes by without a report about a bombing somewhere, or news of a husband killing his wife, a report about children eating wild berries due to hunger. Families are devastated, nations are devastated, and the whole world is in turmoil.

Nothing is certain nowadays. Today you have a good job, tomorrow it's gone. Today you have a beautiful marriage, and tomorrow it is all fallen apart. It is a world of absolute obsolescence. It is a world of broken promises. What or who can we trust when everyday seems to reveal more chaos and moral confusion in its wake?

Day in day out our leaders pledge and promise to seek peace, but that only seems to happen on camera, because deep in the night they plan for wars. Corruption has eaten away what our forefathers fought so hard for. But where can our strength come from? Who can bring about a real and lasting solution to a people who have lost hope in their leaders, a people who have lost hope in themselves, a people who are even losing hope in their God? When the foundations are being destroyed, what can the righteous do?

Jesus Himself prophesied that the end times would be difficult times, and also said in Matthew 24:12 that lawlessness will abound. But we have been promised in Deuteronomy 33:25 that "As your days, so shall your strength be". This means that the bigger our need for spiritual power, the greater the power that God shall provide.

We all at some point go through personal calamities. I consider losing my baby girl the biggest calamity of my life. The bible tells me that God has dominion over all things in heaven and earth, and this means that He had dominion over my broken heart. Through it all, I have learnt to claim God's promise of never leaving me nor forsaking me, and above all, that He remains close to the broken hearted.

Matthew 16:19 - "And I will give you the keys of the kingdom of heaven, and whatever you bind on earth will be bound in heaven, and whatever you loose on earth will be loosed in heaven."

The keys that Jesus is talking about here is that spiritual power that can be available to us once we claim God's promises in our times of need. There are many promises in the word of God, some specific to specific problems, and some universal. The bible says that His promises are yes and amen! What He says he will do, He will do, all you need to do is dare Him to stand by His word, He is always ready and willing.

In the book of Joshua 1:8, the bible has instructed us not to let the Book of the law depart from our mouths, but to meditate on it day and night, so that we may be careful to do everything written in it, then, we will be prosperous and successful. If only we can see that the Lord is proud of us when we are willing to believe in His promises despite all the bad things that are happening to us, that He is so proud of us when we believe in Him despite our disappointments, our heartbreaks and our hurts.

God's promises are so full of power, spiritual power that He wants us to take hold of and apply in our day to day lives. These promises are for every one who has faith enough to believe that God will be true to His word, and that He means exactly what He says. If we can reach out with the hand of faith and claim these promises, God will surely be faithful enough to fulfil every single one of them, so every day we have to activate these promises by reminding ourselves of the promises and feeding our faith.

But you can only know these promises through His word, and only then can you learn how to recognize these promises, and claim them as your own. Claiming these promises is a positive declaration of your own faith and the acknowledgement of God's power and this is what pleases God. He sets His power in motion to answer your prayers.

Below are a few of God's promises that can help us get through these hard times.

Some of my favourite promises in the bible are:

Acts 2:21 - "Whoever calls on the name of the Lord shall be saved"
and

John 14:14 "If you ask anything in my name, I will do it".

In times of great fear, claim the promise in **Isaiah 41:10** where God tells us not to fear for He will be with us; that we should not be dismayed because He is our God, He will strengthen us and help us, and will uphold us in His righteous right hand.

When you look at other people prospering and doing great things and you wonder why you cant be great like them, claim the promise in **Psalms 2:8** that says "Ask of me, and I will make the nations your inheritance, the ends of the earth your possession."

When you are going through a very rough time, claim the promise in **Isaiah 43:2** which says "When you pass through the waters, I will be with you; and when you pass through the rivers, they will not sweep over you. When you walk through the fire, you will not be burned; the flames will not set you ablaze."

Whenever you feel like everything is working against you, claim the promise in **Isaiah 54:17** that says that "no weapon forged against you will prevail and you will refute every tongue that accuses you." There is also another scripture that says that the

173

Lord shall command His angels concerning you, to guard you, so that you may not strike your foot against a stone!

If your body has been afflicted and you feel sick, remember that you can claim healing according to **1st Peter 2:24**, because by His wounds (stripes), we are healed. Also, in **Jeremiah 30:17**, God has promised to restore us and heal us.

When you feel like the Lord has forgotten you, remember to claim the promise in **Isaiah 49:15** that He will not forget you because He has engraved you on the palms of His hands. That even if a mother sometimes forgets her baby, God will never forget you, even in your old age. **Isaiah 46: 4** says that even to your old age and grey hairs, the Lord will sustain you, He has made you and will carry you; and rescue you.

The bible says that the lions may go hungry, but they that trust in the Lord shall lack no good thing. So it does not matter what you are going through today, just get hold of the keys, and claim your promises, and believe that God shall supply all your needs according to His glorious riches in Christ Jesus, **Philippians 4: 19.**

As you continue reminding God of the promises that He has made to you, (yes!, He has given us permission in **Isaiah 43: 26** to put Him into remembrance, to review the past for Him, to argue the matter for Him even as we state our case for innocence), remind Him also that He says that any word that goes out of His mouth shall not return to Him empty, but will accomplish what He desired and achieve the purpose for which He sent it, **Isaiah 55: 11.**

The violent take it, and they take it by force, claim your blessing today, claim your healing today, claim your job today, claim your prosperity today, claim your salvation today, claim your deliverance today, claim your peace today. Claim it! Let God defend His word!

Let your confidence show when you say that you will trust in the Lord whether the sun is shinning and even when the dark cloud settle around you. Choose to believe His promises when the bills have been paid and when your debtors are knocking at your door. His promises are yes! And Amen! Yes, God is what He claims to be! Yes, He will do what He claims He will do.

Matthew 9:29 says that according to your faith, let it be to you. So according to your faith, let God's promises be fulfilled to you.

SCRIPTURE FOCUS

Leviticus 26: 3 - 13

" 'If you follow my decrees and are careful to obey my commands, I will send you rain in its season, and the ground will yield its crops and the trees of the field their fruit. Your threshing will continue until grape harvest and the grape harvest will continue until planting, and you will eat all the food you want and live in safety in your land.

" 'I will grant peace in the land, and you will lie down and no one will make you afraid. I will remove savage beasts from the land, and the sword will not pass through your country. You will pursue your enemies, and they will fall by the sword before you. Five of you will chase a hundred, and a hundred of you will chase ten thousand, and your enemies will fall by the sword before you.

" 'I will look on you with favour and make you fruitful and increase your numbers, and I will keep my covenant with you. You will still be eating last year's harvest when you will have to move it out to make room for the new. I will put my dwelling place [a] among you, and I will not abhor you. I will walk among you and be your God, and you will be my people. I am the Lord your God, who brought you out of Egypt so that you would no longer be slaves to the Egyptians; I broke the bars of your yoke and enabled you to walk with heads held high.

Deuteronomy 28: 1 - 14

If you fully obey the Lord your God and carefully follow all His commands I give you today, the Lord your God will set you high above all the nations on earth. All these blessings will come upon you and accompany you if you obey the Lord your God:

You will be blessed in the city and blessed in the country.

The fruit of your womb will be blessed, and the crops of your land and the young of your livestock—the calves of your herds and the lambs of your flocks.

Your basket and your kneading trough will be blessed.

You will be blessed when you come in and blessed when you go out.

The Lord will grant that the enemies who rise up against you will be defeated before you. They will come at you from one direction but flee from you in seven.

The Lord will send a blessing on your barns and on everything you put your hand to. The Lord your God will bless you in the land He is giving you.

The Lord will establish you as His holy people, as He promised you on oath, if you keep the commands of the Lord your God and walk in His ways. Then all the peoples on earth will see that you are called by the name of the Lord, and they will fear you. The Lord will grant you abundant prosperity—in the fruit of your womb, the young of your livestock and the crops of your ground—in the land He swore to your forefathers to give you.

The Lord will open the heavens, the storehouse of His bounty, to send rain on your land in season and to bless all the work of your hands. You will lend to many nations but will borrow from none. The Lord will make you the head, not the tail. If you pay attention to the commands of the Lord your God that I give you this day and carefully follow them, you will always be at the top, never at the bottom. Do not turn aside from any of the commands I give you today, to the right or to the left, following other gods and serving them.

Chapter 17

Learning To Call Him Jehovah Shalom: The Lord My Peace

*G*ROWING UP AS a young girl, I was a bookworm. I really liked reading, especially stories. Whether reading or whether through a narration, we all know that most stories start out very well, and then somewhere along the way, the narrator says 'suddenly'. The minute you hear 'suddenly' then you know that the story could change dynamically. It means that everything was so peaceful, then suddenly!! What am I trying to say? That even those who have everything their lives going well, they have it all figured out, are always afraid of that 'suddenly' that can occur at any time, without notice, that 'suddenly' that can alter their life stories. So with or without trouble, no one is completely exempt from the fear of the unknown, the fear of what life could surprise us with, the fear of any 'suddenly' that might decide to show up.

If there is a commodity that the whole world desperately needs but is painfully in short supply, and very rare to find, it is peace. Nations are at war with each other, leaders are not getting along, communities are not getting along with each other, families are not peaceful, and we are not getting along with each other. There is a lack of peace that can transcend nationalities, tribes, social class, race, gender, ethnicity, culture, a peace that can transcend opinions.

Some countries believe they are small deities that have the unquestioned right to rule other countries. There is a lack of peace that our politicians, even with all their promises cannot be able to offer us. We are not even at peace with creation itself! Hurricanes, earthquakes, floods, they have all teamed up to destroy mankind! From where shall we find peace?

People are going through tough, turbulent times, and there is so much heartache, so much suffering and pain. How can one remain peaceful when everything is spinning out of control, how can one remain peaceful in the face of trials tribulations and temptations? How can one keep their peace in the midst of storms and troubled waters? How will my peace remain with me in the face of anger, fear, anxiety, mockery and rejection? Where will I get that true peace that will remain secure no matter what I go through? From where can we get that feeling of sweet comforting peace that can take away all our worries? Where can we call our place of refuge? A place that can be a safe harbour from pain, suffering, and the anguish that is all around us?

In a society where everyone is becoming increasingly stressed-out, and people are continually living in a state of anxiety, a society facing health problems, threats of terrorism, violence within and without our homes, parenting challenges, difficult marriages, financial challenges, moral decay, and not to mention a world that is advancing so fast technologically that it leaves one in a continuous state of dizziness, where can we find peace? Where can we find stability?

That is why 'Shalom' is most probably the first word someone will tell you once you step into Israel, and as well, the last word on your departure. It is their way of wishing one another peace, and it has now been accepted worldwide as a form of greeting, the same way you would say 'hallo'. Its origin is in the book of Joshua chapter 6, when the children of Israel rebelled against God, and God handed them over to the Midianites who oppressed them for seven years, until Gideon cried to the Lord for help. God sent an angel to Gideon to tell him that He would use him to save the Israelites from the Midianites. Gideon was very afraid because he was the least in his family, and furthermore, his clan was the weakest. But the Lord told him, "Peace. Do not be afraid, you are not going to die." It is here that Gideon built an altar and called it "Shalom, The Lord is Peace."

John 14:27 "Peace I leave with you, My peace I give to you; not as the world gives do I give to you. Let not your heart be troubled, neither let it be afraid.

Symbolically, peace is represented by a white dove. When God saved Noah and his family from the floods, a dove came to him carrying an olive branch on its beak and Noah knew that it the floods had ended, that it was once again safe to live on the land, that everything was well.

Peace is a fruit of the Holy Spirit. It is that harmonious relationship between one and another, harmonious relationship between God and man; it is the quietness of surroundings, both external and internal. When God created mankind, He intended us to live peacefully, He wanted us to have life and have life in abundance. There is no way we can have the abundance of life if we are not peaceful.

However, one of the gifts God gave us a will to choose between good and evil, right and wrong, love and hate. He has given us the freedom to make decisions as we deem fit, and to use our consciences to make judgments. So we do as we please, we make our own rules, and we ignore His rules. He gave us a choice to either obey Him or disobey Him. But because of man's sinful nature that has been passed down from our forefathers, man found Himself separated from God, not at peace with God. Isaiah 59:2 says that "... your iniquities have separated you from your God..." we have shut God out of our lives. We have distanced ourselves from God.

The initial access, closeness as well as fellowship with the only source of true peace have been broken down. God never intended for us to live in a world that lacks peace, He never meant for us to live so anxious about life every day. His intention was that we stay close to His heart and enjoy the abundance of His promises. But in our endless efforts to seek and pursue peace, we have followed all the wrong methods and ways. The book of Proverbs 14:12 says that there is a way that seems right to a man but in the end it leads to death.

We have tried to close the separation gap between us and God using bridges that cannot guarantee us that inner peace. We have invested our time, money as well as emotions on superficial things which we think will make us happy in life, and give us peace. We think that having good jobs, wealth, family and friends will give us peace but we are wrong. All these are material things that will make us happy but cannot guarantee us peace during our toughest moments. They are just but material things that will mount pressure on our lives and give us so much stress and bring so much distraction that our thoughts will more often than not be pulled away from our God, the only one who is able to give us true peace.

The only bridge that can reconcile us with God and give us everlasting peace is the cross of Jesus Christ. It is through His death on the cross that mankind was once again reconciled with God. 1st Timothy 2:5 tells us that there is one God, and one mediator between God and man, the man Jesus Christ. When Christ was born, and even long before He was born, it was prophesied in Isaiah 9: 6 that the prince of peace had come, that the ultimate peace had come. True peace will come from getting reconciled with God through our Lord Jesus Christ, by accepting the gift of salvation that he offered us on the cross.

During His ministry, He promised us that His peace would stay with us even after He was gone. John 14: 27 says "Peace I leave with you; my peace I give you. I do not give you as the world gives..." The worldly things can give us superficial peace for some time, but this peace can end in a twinkling of an eye. Many have relied on the 'peace' that comes from our material possessions only to lead very miserable lives. But the peace that God gives us is the peace that comes from having faith in Him, a faith that comes from trusting Him, a peace that comes from yielding to the will of God and letting Him be God. It is the peace that comes from approaching Him with an open heart and an open mind; approaching Him the way a child approaches his father, knowing that his father will not lead Him astray.

It is only in trusting the Lord with all your heart, with all your soul, with all your mind, with everything in you, and leaning not in your own understanding that you will find peace. It is only in when you yield totally and submit to Him, leaving yourself with no other option but God that you will find true, perfect peace. The refuge that the Lord has promised you is the solace of His love, the comfort from the envelop of His arms, and the peace that will fill your heart.

So you say that you have found salvation in Jesus Christ but you still have not experienced peace, and every time there is a storm in your life, the one thing that is hardest to find is peace? The 12 men who were closest to Jesus Himself during His earthly ministry could echo your feelings. In the gospel of Mark chapter 4, Jesus told His disciples, "let us go over to the other side". When they were in the boat, the bible says that a furious squall came up and the waves broke over the boat, so that it was nearly swamped. All this time Jesus was sleeping, so the disciples went to Him and asked if He didn't care if they drowned. Here, we have a case where the Lord says let us do this, but somehow, a storm sets in. So when the Lord said that they go over the other side, and the storm came, it seems like the disciples did not take Jesus at His word, that they would get to the other side.

Just the same way you might be overwhelmed with your physical conditions and circumstances, the same way you feel like you are swamped with responsibilities that see totally beyond your capabilities, the same way you feel that you are to drown in a sea of debts, is the same exact way that the disciples felt when the boat threatened to capsize. The disciples must have tried to remember all the lessons and the tricks they had learned about sailing, but they surely had forgotten what the Lord Himself had said. Are you in the same situation? Trying so hard to remember the rules of survival that you hardly remember what the Lord says?

When Jesus got up, He rebuked wind and commanded the waves to be still, and then the wind died down and it was completely calm. And then Jesus asked His disciples, "Why are you so afraid? Do you still have no faith?' The disciples were terrified and asked each other who Jesus was, that even the wind and the waves obey Him. Have you just like the disciples been too busy looking for a natural solution that you have completely neglected the supernatural word from Him who has the authority to calm a storm? Or is it that you remember what the Lord says but just don't take Him at His word? Or could it be that you still do not know that Jesus has authority to command the wind and the waves?

Philippians 4:7 - ". . . and the peace of God, which surpasses all understanding, will guard your hearts and minds through Christ Jesus."

No matter what you are going through, you can have peace in knowing that Jesus, the prince of peace will never leave you nor forsake you. You can have peace from knowing that the Prince of Peace arose from death to execute His promise of peace that surpasses all understanding. It's only from Christ that you can get a sense of calmness, relaxation and peace. Only the Lord God is our safe haven. There is no one else, not even our pastors can give us true peace because some have become so greedy and have continually enriched themselves by misinterpreting God's Holy word instead of preaching the true gospel of Jesus Christ.

Our government is not a safe haven either, if anything, all it continues to do is give us more problems than solutions. If you are looking for peace from a fellow man, then the bible says that you are cursed. Jeremiah 17: 5 says clearly that cursed is the man that trusts in man, and makes flesh his arm, and whose heart departs from the Lord.

As children of God, we have the promise of peace to have and to keep. Philippians 4: 7 says that "And the peace of God, which transcends all understanding will guard your hearts and your mind in Christ Jesus" . And not only are we called to have peace, but we are also called to be peacemakers. Colossians 3:15 urges us to let the peace of Christ rule in our hearts, since we are members of one body and we are called to peace. It is up to you to therefore search your heart and ask yourself if you are a peacemaker or a peace-breaker.

What I want is the kind of peace that made Jesus sleep on the boat during a stormy night while His disciples were worried sick, the kind of peace that will see me through financial hardships, sickness, and other life's frustrations. I want the kind of peace that will make me smile when my situation dictates that I should be sighing.

SHALOM!

SCRIPTURE FOCUS

Ezekiel 34:25-26

"And I will make with them a Covenant Of Peace, and will cause the evil beasts to cease out of the land: and they shall dwell safely in the wilderness, and sleep in the woods. Moreover I will make a Covenant Of Peace with them; it shall be an Everlasting Covenant with them: and I will place them, and multiply them, and will set My sanctuary in the midst of them for evermore."

Ephesians. 2:14-15

"For He is our Peace, Who hath made both one, and hath broken down the middle wall of partition between us; having abolished in His flesh the enmity, even the law of commandments contained in ordinances; for to make in Himself of twain one new man, so making peace"

Colossians 3:15

"And let the peace of God rule in your hearts, to the which also ye are called in one body; and be ye thankful."

John 14:27

"Peace I leave with you, My peace I give unto you: not as the world giveth, give I unto you. Let not your heart be troubled, neither let it be afraid."

Chapter 18

Learning To Call Him Jehovah Rophe (Rapha): The Lord My Healer

I AM SURE THAT every one of us has gotten sick at some point in their lives; we have lost loved ones to sickness. There are those who are confined to bed right now, those needing intensive care. Even in the olden days, sickness was so much a part of people's lives, only difference being that today we are so blessed with medical training and medical apparatus. Diagnosis and treatment are so much easier in today's world.

God is not the author of sickness. If we look back in the book of Genesis, man's willful disobedience to God did not only bring separation from God but it also brought about physical death. We therefore inherited both spiritual and physical death from our father Adam, as well as sickness and disease. But God in His loving kindness and mercies has continually healed us.

In the book of Exodus 15: 22-26, we are told that after the Israelites crossed the Red Sea after fleeing from Egypt, they came across a place called Marah, where they could not drink the water as it was bitter. They complained to Moses, who in turn cried out to God. The Lord showed him a piece of wood and instructed him to throw it into the water. The water turned sweet again.

It was here that the Lord told them, "if you listen carefully to the voice of the Lord your God and do what is right in His eyes, if you pay attention to His commands, and keep all His decrees, I will not bring on you any of the diseases I brought on the Egyptians, for I am the Lord who heals you". This is a declaration of the power of Jehovah Rophe, the Lord our healer. The name 'rophe' means to heal, to restore, and to cure.

1Peter 2:24 - "... who Himself bore our sins in His own body on the tree, that we, having died to sins, might live for righteousness- by whose stripes you were healed."

During His short public ministry, Jesus spent quite a considerable amount of time healing those that needed healing, one by one. Even though He was always surrounded by great crowds, He was never too busy to minister healing. We also see Him commissioning His disciples in Matthew 10: 7-8, that they should heal the sick, among other things.

Through His substotionary death for us, Jesus bore the results of all our sins, including sickness and disease. Because Jesus purchased our healing by being stripped, it is therefore God's will that we be healed.

In the book of Jeremiah 30:17, the Lord promises to restore us and to heal our wounds. During the calling of Matthew, one of Jesus' disciples, we see Jesus saying that it is not the healthy who need the doctor but the sick. He is not only talking about physical healing, but He is talking about spiritual and emotional healing.

We are all sinners in need of spiritual healing. The church is the first stop for our healing, it is God's hospital. He who took up our infirmities and carried our sorrows, He who was pierced for our transgressions and crushed for our iniquities is faithful to cleanse us of all our sins, and heal us spiritually. Nobody can heal our spiritual evils except God Himself.

Maybe you are in a relationship that needs healing, well the first step is forgiveness because forgiveness sets in motion a process of healing. God will heal your broken heart no matter how overwhelming the hurt may be. He will reach into your deep wounds with a touch of healing.

Sometimes the healing may be immediately, sometimes the healing may be very slow, and other times it may also be very dramatic. Most times, the healing may be through doctors and medicine. We serve a healing God! A God who has compassion for His people, a God who by His stripes we are healed.

Not only is God the healer of our physical bodies, but He is also the healer of our hearts, our emotions, our spirits; He heals all aspects of a man's being. Maybe you have been hurt emotionally, maybe you are going through some pain spiritually and you feel that you cannot take it anymore. Well, there is some good news for you. Jesus is our great physician, He will give you spiritual restoration. His healing hand will reach deep and touch your deep hurts.

I believe in faith healing, and even though sometimes I may not have enough faith myself, I know that sometimes God heals us on the account of someone else's faith, especially when He wants to get us started on our own faith. Hebrews 11:1 says that faith is the substance of things hoped for, the evidence of things not seen.

Are you struggling with doubts about healing? Choose to believe in Jesus' healing, He is our great physician, He sees every cell, every muscle, every bone in our bodies. His healing is once and for all. Healing is yours, just take God at His word and you will be healed. Experience Jehovah Rophe!

SCRIPTURE FOCUS

Exodus 15:26

...If you will diligently listen to the voice of the Lord your God, and do that which is right in His eyes, and give ear to His commandments and keep all His statutes, I will put none of the diseases on you that I put on the Egyptians, for I am the Lord, your healer."

Deuteronomy 7:15

And the Lord will take away from you all sickness, and none of the evil diseases of Egypt, which you knew, will He inflict on you, but He will lay them on all who hate you.

Exodus 23:25-26

You shall serve the Lord your God, and He will bless your bread and your water, and I will take sickness away from among you. None shall miscarry or be barren in your land; I will fulfil the number of your days.

Chapter 19

Learning To Call Him Jehovah Nissi: The Lord My Banner

*I*F THERE HAVE been years in my life when I needed my God to show Himself strong and true as Jehovah my banner, Jehovah my victory, it was the last few years, a time when everything was at war with me? I fought lack, war, disease, depression, joblessness and loneliness. I was tossed to and fro by forces some of which I did not even understand. I found myself fighting unexpected battles that I had no control over.

I learnt that the enemy is never pleased whenever we make a conscience effort to seek the Lord. It is at that time that the devil mounts war on us. He throws very fiery darts at us and at those times there are plenty of chances for us to be defeated. There is a battle raging for our souls and we cannot win the battle without God's help.

The Israelites went through the same in the wilderness. After crossing the Red Sea, they started wondering in the desert. It was there that the Amalekites came against them. Exodus 17: 8-16 gives us an account of what happened. Moses asked Joshua to lead the Israelites into battle as he, Moses, went to the mountain to pray.

When Moses was praying, as long as he held his hands up, the Israelites were winning, but whenever he lowered his hands, the Amalekites were winning. It reached a point when Moses got tired, and Aaron and Hur had to hold his hands up, one on one side and one on the other. At the end of the day the Israelites won the battle.

It was here that Moses built an altar which in those days was used to mark and remember important events. He called the altar 'Jehovah Nissi', meaning the Lord is my banner. A banner or a flag is a symbol of victory, it gives a sense of identity, belonging and pride. On so many occasions we have seen our athletes raise up the Kenyan flag as a symbol of victory. Every time a Kenyan wins a race, the Kenyan flag is raised.

And just like an athlete identifies with their country using a flag, so are the children of God expected to identify with God as their banner because our victory is only in Him. With Jehovah as your banner, He will fight your battles for you and lead you to victory. From Exodus to Deuteronomy to Chronicles to Joshua to Samuel to Psalms to Proverbs, and throughout the bible, God has constantly reminded us that the battle belongs to Him.

It doesn't matter what kind of battle you are going through, he will win it for you. Just like Moses, all you have to do is raise your hands in prayer, and when you feel like you cannot continue raising them anymore, ask your friends to help you raise them up. The bible also tells us that Christ who is seated at the right hand of God, is making intercession for us. Call upon Jehovah Nissi and you shall surely see the deliverance of the Lord.

Battles will come and opposition will arise, but when you are hard pressed in the battlefield, look over your shoulder and you will see the banner that is over you, reminding you that victory will be yours. Chose to focus on the victory ahead. The bible tells us that our adversary is much stronger than us, but with God as our banner, our victory is guaranteed. No weapon that is formed against us shall prosper.

Does your circumstance seem impossible? Are you ready to throw in the towel? If you allow the Lord to fight your battles, He will turn your fear into faith, your unbelief into belief. Choose today to make the Lord God your banner, your victory, your conqueror, let Him be your focus point in times of trouble. Let Him be a banner of encouragement to fight on.

Song of Songs (also called Song of Solomon) 2:4 tells us that His banner over us is love. In Him you will find refuge. In Him your banner will always fly high as a sign of the victory that He will give you. As a child of the most high God, you have access to a warrior who has never lost in battle.

When you are facing frustration and defeat, and feel like the Lord is taking too long to win the battle for you, and you are may be tempted to fight the battle yourself. Do not, Genesis 14:14 tells you to be still, to hold your peace. Just take courage my friend because your redemption is near, your banner is flying high!!

The name of the Lord has sure been my refuge, for every time I would lift His name as a banner, He was always there to remind me that victory was on its way. This is why I have decided that I am not going to look around me lest I be distracted, I am not going to look within me lest I be distressed, I am not going to look back lest I be defeated, nor am I going to look down lest I be discouraged, instead I choose today to look up to my banner so that I may be delivered, I chose to look unto Jesus so that I may be delighted!

SCRIPTURE FOCUS

Exodus 17: 8-16

The Amalekites came and attacked the Israelites at Rephidim. Moses said to Joshua, "Choose some of our men and go out to fight the Amalekites. Tomorrow I will stand on top of the hill with the staff of God in my hands."

So Joshua fought the Amalekites as Moses had ordered, and Moses, Aaron and Hur went to the top of the hill. As long as Moses held up his hands, the Israelites were winning, but whenever he lowered his hands, the Amalekites were winning. When Moses' hands grew tired, they took a stone and put it under him and he sat on it. Aaron and Hur held his hands up—one on one side, one on the other—so that his hands remained steady till sunset. So Joshua overcame the Amalekite army with the sword.

Then the LORD said to Moses, "Write this on a scroll as something to be remembered and make sure that Joshua hears it, because I will completely blot out the memory of Amalek from under heaven."

Moses built an altar and called it The LORD is my Banner. He said, "For hands were lifted up to the throne of the LORD. The LORD will be at war against the Amalekites from generation to generation."

Chapter 20

Learning To Appreciate The Wonder Of Creation

"O Lord, my God, when I in awesome wonder,
consider all the works thy hands have made;
I see the stars, I hear the roaring thunder,
Thy power throughout the universe displayed..."

THIS IS A favourite tune that brings me to my knees - just marvelling at the wonder of creation, God's infinite wisdom and power. My second chance at life has really made me appreciative of everything around me and every one of God's creation. I will never be the same again. I appreciate life so much. I no longer take things for granted. I purposed in my heart NEVER to see life as a routine but to see it as a daily miracle. I have learnt that being happy does not come from having a lot, but by appreciating twice what I already have, even as I try to make life better. I have learnt to see God in His creation.

Do you ever look at the radiant smile of a baby and see God? Do you look at the beautiful sunset as you enjoy your evening, and you can't help but hold your breath as you glimpse into God's presence? That is because every tree, every flower, every mountain, every river, every ocean, every leaf and every butterfly bears God's imprint. Genesis 1:1 says that in the beginning God created the heavens and the earth (and everything in them).

I believe that there are many ways in which God speaks to mankind. One way is through His holy word, and another is through the masterpiece of creation. Even when God is not speaking to us through His Word, the eloquence of His creation just compels us to be still and stand in silent wonder before our God. The very act of meditating on God's power should bring us into a place of worship, a place of humility as we marvel at the greatness of our creator.

We need to realize that mankind cannot survive without God's other creation; we are totally dependent upon the fruitfulness of His creation for our health and livelihood. What would happen if God shut up the heavens and there was no rain? Psalms 104: 14-15 says: *"He causes the grass to grow for the cattle, and vegetation for the service of man, that He may bring forth food from the earth, and wine that makes glad the heart of man, oil to make His face shine, and bread which strengthens man's heart."*

Do you remember life in the rural village when you would enjoy the morning dew as you walked to school? It is most unfortunate that after we have become urbanized, we have lost that divine connection that we had with God's creation. The skyscrapers have blocked our view from God's beautiful heaven, the numerous factories have polluted the air so much that we no longer remember how it feels like to breathe some fresh air. When was the last time you took time to admire the stars at night? Am sure that for most of us, the last time we saw a flower was on the Internet, or that screen saver on our computers.

Not only should we enjoy God's creation, we are also charged with the responsibility of taking care of it. In the book of Genesis, we see how God took man (Adam), and put him in the garden of Eden to tend and keep it. Man, who is the crown of God's creation as He was made in the likeness of God, was given dominion over the works of God's hands. This stewardship should make us honour His name as we use and develop His creation.

Remember, all that God's creation wants from you is the sheer awareness of its full and rich presence. I long for the day when mankind will look at a tree and its flowers and proclaim, "Holy Holy Holy is the Lord God Almighty!" I long for the day when we will be compelled back to the path from which we have strayed, a path that will do away with our self imposed blindness, and in turn start appreciating and celebrating the wonder of creation.

I long for the day when we shall gladly appreciate the singing of the birds, the fluttering of the butterflies, the budding of the flowers; a day when we shall go back to the innocence of our childhood. I long for the day when we shall greet the morning sunshine with smiles and thankfulness. Psalms 19:1 says, *"The heavens declare the glory of God, and the firmament shows His handiwork",* because God is the greatest Master of them all.

As God's creation continues to amaze us, remember that if He takes so much care of the birds of the air, He cares for us even more. He intended for us to live happily, carefree, enjoying life, as His creation and with His other creation.

Nothing in this world can give us as much peace and joy as appreciating God's creation. And although man may be trying to outdo God in everything, he will never come close. A joke is told of a scientist who challenged God that he (the scientist) has finally figured out a way to create a man. God then asked the man to explain how to do it. "Well, we can take plain dirt, form it into the likeness of you, and breathe life into it, thus creating man" says the scientist. "That's very interesting, please show me how", says God. So the scientist bends down to the earth and starts to mould the soil into the shape of man. "NO, NO!" God interrupts, "Get your own dirt!"

SCRIPTURE FOCUS

Genesis 1:1, 31

"In the beginning God created the heavens and the earth...
God saw all that he had made, and it was very good."

Nehemiah 9:6

"You made the heavens, even the highest heavens, and all their
starry host, the earth and all that is on it, the seas and all that
is in them. You give life to everything, and the multitudes of
heaven worship you."

Psalm 65:9-13

"You care for the land and water it; you enrich it abundantly.
The streams of God are filled with water to provide the
people with grain, for so you have ordained it. You drench its
furrows and level its ridges; you soften it with showers and
bless its crops. You crown the year with your bounty, and your
carts overflow with abundance. The grasslands of the desert
overflow; the hills are clothed with gladness. The meadows
are covered with flocks and the valleys are mantled with grain;
they shout for joy and sing."

Psalm 104:10-14

"He makes springs pour water into the ravines; it flows between
the mountains. They give water to all the beasts of the field; the
wild donkeys quench their thirst. The birds of the air nest by the
waters; they sing among the branches. He waters the mountains
from His upper chambers; the earth is satisfied by the fruit of
His work. He makes grass grow for the cattle, and plants for man
to cultivate-bringing forth food from the earth."

Chapter 21

Destiny Now Beckons

*M*Y JOURNEY FROM a quiet, peaceful life to a turbulent and rough storm has been one I would like to liken to a potters furnace. The Lord in His own way had to break me into pieces, small pieces so that He could mold and shape me back to the person He created me to be. He had to break my hardened heart and soften it for His work. As beautiful as my life may have looked to an outsider, there was a lot of work that needed to be done on the inside.

Growing up in a family where I was not really accepted made me accumulate a lot of anger and resentment on the inside. As much as I tried to forgive those who had hurt me in my childhood, I just couldn't get myself to do it. As a grown up, I tried to escape any memories of my childhood as best as I could. This meant a disconnection with my family. I tried to just be 'alone'. As much as I loved my mother and my siblings, I avoided visiting home because of the ugly memories that would be rekindled by others.

On my own, I started my new life, a life without family, a life just with friends and colleagues. It wasn't easy trying to fit in with friends though I always appeared to have it all together. I always had very good grades in school, I remember I was leading in our school in the KCPE in our year. I got admitted to a very good national high school, performed well, and the rest is history. Even when I started working, I was always good at whatever I laid my hands on. It is from here that I got favour with various people and ended up with good jobs.

But even with a seemingly successful career, I was still a very angry person. I had developed sarcasm as a defence mechanism; I was very sensitive, always over reading what people said to me, wondering whether they were out to hurt me. So whenever I suspected that someone was out to hurt me, I would always switch on my "I'll-get-you-before-you-get-me" mentality.

Life didn't make things any easier for me. I had dreamt of a perfect love life, but I had an endless cycle of temporary relationships. A few failed relationships and I declared to myself that I was NEVER going to get married. I can say that my decision never to get married is what triggered everything that has happened so far. I say this because it is the reason I left church, in as far as work and studies had a part to play in me not attending church, part of it was largely because I never wanted to get married, yet I wanted a baby. And so the only way I felt I would get a baby outside marriage and get away with it was by forsaking church and backing off completely from the fellowship of other believers. I did not want anyone questioning my decision, not even God.

So I went ahead and got pregnant, not really with an intention to get married and have a family, all I wanted was a baby, period. And though at some time I may have considered marriage during my pregnancy, deep inside I knew I was never going to tolerate nonsense from a man, so at the slightest provocation I would always want to change my mind. The more I tried to force my own will into my life and push God aside, the more I walked away from God.

My career was going very well until I got the accident that killed my daughter, reality with its ugly consequences set in, and the rest as you now know, is as I have narrated in this book. From there it has been a season of loss, from loss of my daughter, to loss of a prestigious job, to loss of property, loss of finances, it has been a period where I lost everything I had worked for in the last 10 years and more. I was at a point where it just could not get worse. I was at a place where I no longer had any control over anything. Everything in my life was shaken and torn apart.

And just like that God had my full attention!

Jeremiah 2:13 - "My people have committed two sins: They have forsaken me the spring of living water, and they have dug their own cisterns, broken cisterns that cannot hold water."

I do not blame anyone for anything, I am the one who moved away from God's care and set myself up for life's bitter winds. I had ignored God for years. This and more I was guilty of. The Lord in His infinite wisdom has allowed circumstances to break me into pieces; I have been brought down to my knees, sending me to a refiner's fire that He talks about in Malachi, to purify me, to cleanse me from all the impurities that had clogged my heart and to destroy the rebellious spirit in me. I had to swallow my pride until there was no more pride left for me to swallow, and then turn my life back to Jesus.

I have over the last few years been in a state where I cannot go back to 'my Egypt' since He made sure to destroy it, yet I also could not move on to 'my Canaan' since I was not ready. Am now in the process of being the person that God intended me to be, and even though I am far from being perfect, I am now like clay in His hands, being molded into His vessel, and often soaking in His presence so as to keep soft. I have learnt the hard way that it is better that the Lord corrects you when you are still 'soft', than to break you into pieces when you are already hardened.

He has so far restored my broken cup and filled it to overflowing just as He has promised in Psalms 23:5. He surely has re-build the ancient ruins and restored the places long devastated. He has and still is working on my heart, and though my journey to wholeness has not been fast, He has given me the strength and wisdom to keep moving forward.

The process of making me into the vessel that He wanted me to be has been painful, very painful indeed, but it has been worth it all. He has made me die to myself, and though I am still a work in progress, I am sure that when He looks at me now, He sees a vessel that is worthy of His use. God is now giving me a new beginning. I know that once He is done molding me, many will see the real me, the person that God created me to be. I am now hidden in Him and I have no apologies to make for that. I am certain that He will shelter me under His wings.

John 15:16 - "You did not choose Me, but I chose you and appointed you that you should go and bear fruit, and that your fruit should remain, that whatever you ask the Father in My name He may give you."

I never imagined that someone as broken as I was could ever be used of God. But God proved me wrong and proved to me that just because I had given up on Him, it didn't mean that He gave up on me. As I now conclude this book, I am thankful to God that He continues to use me to encourage others. It is because of my story that I can walk alongside those who are going through the same path as I have been. It is because of my story that I can understand their broken hearts. It is because of my story that I am a better and not a bitter person.

If it wasn't for the pain that I have gone through I would not be the refined person that I am today. That is the reason I decided not just to write about my pain, but to emphasize more on the role that the pain has played in molding me. It is not easy to let your life be an open book, but if it will help someone get through what they are going through, and possibly understand that there is a bigger purpose, then by all means let my life be an open book. I cannot hold on to my pain, but I will use it to defy the odds to achieve what God has ordained for me.

When David was growing up in His father's house, His father did not see much use of him except to tender his sheep in the desert. It must have been in that desert that David learnt to compose those Psalms. Just like David, it is in my desert that I have learnt to compose my own pieces of writing that encourage others. It was in prison that Joseph sharpened his skills at interpreting dreams. I believe that this, writing, is part of my destiny, and destiny beckons now! God has birthed in me new dreams and new visions. I can confidently say that am now in my last days of my journey through my wilderness, I am no longer an Egyptian slave, I can see Canaan from where I am. My blessing is just around the corner.

I don't know what stage of your life you are at now, but I would like to urge you to look at your life and ask yourself if like me, you have forsaken His living water and dug your own cisterns. Maybe you have not come to a place of brokenness like I did, but you do not have to wait until then. Choose to bring your heart to Him today, for He has said in John 15: 16 that He chose you and appointed you to go and bear fruit that will last. If He did it for me, He will do it for you!

SCRIPTURE FOCUS

Isaiah 61

The Spirit of the Lord GOD is upon me; because the LORD hath anointed me to preach good tidings unto the meek; He hath sent me to bind up the brokenhearted, to proclaim liberty to the captives, and the opening of the prison to them that are bound;

To proclaim the acceptable year of the LORD, and the day of vengeance of our God; to comfort all that mourn;

To appoint unto them that mourn in Zion, to give unto them beauty for ashes, the oil of joy for mourning, the garment of praise for the spirit of heaviness; that they might be called trees of righteousness, the planting of the LORD, that He might be glorified.

And they shall build the old wastes, they shall raise up the former desolations, and they shall repair the waste cities, the desolations of many generations.

And strangers shall stand and feed your flocks, and the sons of the alien shall be your plowmen and your vine dressers.

But ye shall be named the Priests of the LORD: men shall call you the Ministers of our God: ye shall eat the riches of the Gentiles, and in their glory shall ye boast yourselves.

For your shame ye shall have double; and for confusion they shall rejoice in their portion: therefore in their land they shall possess the double: everlasting joy shall be unto them.

For I the LORD love judgment, I hate robbery for burnt offering; and I will direct their work in truth, and I will make an everlasting covenant with them.

And their seed shall be known among the Gentiles, and their offspring among the people: all that see them shall acknowledge them, that they are the seed which the LORD hath blessed.

I will greatly rejoice in the LORD, my soul shall be joyful in my God; for He hath clothed me with the garments of salvation, He hath covered me with the robe of righteousness, as a bridegroom decketh himself with ornaments, and as a bride adorneth herself with her jewels.

For as the earth bringeth forth her bud, and as the garden causeth the things that are sown in it to spring forth; so the Lord GOD will cause righteousness and praise to spring forth before all the nations.

THE BEGINNING!...

... of destiny,

... of a purposeful life!

www.ingramcontent.com/pod-product-compliance
Lightning Source LLC
LaVergne TN
LVHW051628080426
835511LV00016B/2230